THE IDENTITY CRASH

How to Redefine Your Worth in the Age of AI

Disclaimer

This book is intended for informational and educational purposes only. The views, ideas, and opinions expressed are those of the author and are based on research, professional experience, and interpretation at the time of publication. While every effort has been made to ensure accuracy, the author makes no representations or warranties regarding the completeness, reliability, or suitability of the information contained herein.

This book does not constitute legal, financial, psychological, career, or other professional advice. Readers should consult qualified professionals before making decisions related to their careers, finances, personal development, or other matters discussed in this book.

Discussions regarding artificial intelligence, automation, workplace transformation, and future trends reflect current developments and informed projections. Technology and market conditions evolve rapidly, and no guarantees are made regarding future outcomes, predictions, or results.

By reading this book, you acknowledge that you are solely responsible for your own decisions, actions, and results. The author shall not be held liable for any loss, damage, or consequences arising from the use or misuse of the information presented.

Cover Photo: Cover artwork created using AI-assisted tools and original design direction by the author. Inspired by Michelangelo's David (public domain).

ISBN: 979-8-9868976-3-9

Publisher
Unitech International LLC
561-214-5757

THE IDENTITY CRASH

How to Redefine Your Worth in the Age of AI

✦✦✦

"It is not the strongest of the species that survives, nor the most intelligent; it is the one most responsive to change."

— Charles Darwin

"We shall not cease from exploration, and the end of all our exploring will be to arrive where we started and know the place for the first time."

— T.S. Eliot

"The machine does not isolate man from the great problems of nature but plunges him more deeply into them."

— Antoine de Saint-Exupéry

CONTENTS

✦ ✦ ✦

A NOTE ON THIS BOOK

✦ ✦ ✦

The arguments in these pages first began to crystallize for me not in a think tank or a university seminar, but in a series of conversations I had with people who were, in the most ordinary sense of the word, struggling. A graphic designer who had spent eighteen years building an aesthetic sensibility that felt utterly her own, watching a client generate in thirty seconds something that would have taken her a week. A radiologist who had devoted a decade to the subtle art of reading imaging scans, now reviewing AI-generated preliminary reports that were, in measurable ways, more accurate than his unaided interpretations. A novelist whose agent told her, with evident discomfort, that the market had fundamentally changed and that 'AI-assisted' manuscripts were now flooding the submission pipeline at a pace that defied comprehension.

None of these people were catastrophizing or being precious about the value of their work. They were intelligent, adaptive, and professionally accomplished individuals who were grappling honestly with a genuine and unprecedented situation: the discovery that the specific cognitive capacities they had spent years developing were no longer as rare, as valued, or as definitive of their professional identity as they had believed.

This book is written for them. And for the many millions of people who are, at this moment, experiencing versions of the same discovery — whether they have named it yet or not.

A word about what this book is and is not. It is not a technology primer. It does not attempt to explain how large language models work, or to map the competitive landscape of the AI industry, or to predict which jobs will be automated by which date. These are important topics that other books address with greater technical expertise than I can bring to them.

What this book attempts is something different: to understand the psychological, philosophical, and spiritual dimensions of the transition we are undergoing. To ask not, 'what is happening to the economy?' but 'what is happening to us?' — to the people inside the economy, the people whose sense of purpose, significance, and identity is bound up in the work that the economy is rapidly transforming.

The answers this book offers are not comfortable. They require a genuine rethinking of assumptions that most of us have never consciously examined — assumptions about what makes a life valuable, what constitutes a meaningful day, and what we owe ourselves and each other in a world that is being reshaped faster than our hearts can follow.

But they are, I believe, true. And eventually, the truth — however demanding — is more useful than the comfort of pretending that nothing fundamental has changed.

INTRODUCTION

The Great Monday Morning Silence

The transition did not begin with a roar of engines or the sudden appearance of humanoid robots on our doorsteps. It did not announce itself with a presidential address or a breaking news chyron. It crept in on padded feet, wearing the face of convenience, wrapped in the language of optimization. It arrived the way all great disruptions eventually arrive — not as a storm, but as a slow, almost imperceptible shift in the weather.

It began with the quiet hum of servers and the soft, blue glow of screens. It began in the small hours of the morning, when data centers the size of small towns started processing more information than all human civilization had generated in the previous ten thousand years combined. It began, in the truest sense, long before most of us were paying attention.

For decades, we have lived as devoted parishioners in a global, secular religion. Call it The Church of the Grind. This is a world in which human identity is not merely influenced by labor — it is entirely forged in its fires. A world where 'busyness' has become the ultimate civic virtue, where the hustle is not merely what you do but who you are, and where the terrifying absence of a task feels less like rest and more like a moral failing. We have built careers, relationships, and entire self-concepts on the granite foundation of our professional utility.

We are now entering The Identity Crash.

This is the moment — already underway, already irreversible — where the cognitive tasks we spent years, decades, and fortunes mastering are being performed by algorithms with a speed and precision that no human body can match. The code you spent three years learning to write is being generated in seconds. The legal brief that took a junior associate a weekend of sleepless labor is being drafted in minutes. The medical diagnosis that required fifteen years of residency and fellowship is being suggested by a pattern-recognition engine that has 'read' more case studies than any single physician could absorb in three lifetimes.

This is not science fiction. This is Tuesday morning.

And it is on exactly that kind of unremarkable Tuesday morning — when the inbox is empty, the algorithm has handled the reports, and you sit before a screen with nothing urgent to do — that the crash begins. Not with a bang, but with a silence. A great, echoing Monday morning silence that is louder than any alarm clock you have ever set.

The question that silence asks is unbearable in its simplicity:

Who are you when you have nothing to do?

This book exists because that question needs an answer. Not a philosophical abstraction or a self-help platitude, but a genuine, earned, and practical answer grounded in the reality of what it means to be a human animal navigating a world being rapidly reshaped by non-human intelligence.

The pages that follow are a journey through the psychology, sociology, neuroscience, and philosophy of what it means to locate your worth in an age that is actively delegitimizing the traditional sources of that worth. We will explore how we got here — how labor became identity, and how identity became vulnerability. We will diagnose the specific pathologies of the transition: the bore-out, the Uselessness Syndrome, the Dopamine Trap. And we will map a route forward — not a retreat into Luddite fantasy, but an advance into a richer, more authentic, and more human way of being alive.

How to Read This Book

This book is organized in three broad movements. The first movement — Chapters One through Three — is diagnostic. It traces the historical and psychological origins of the crisis we are experiencing, from the Industrial Revolution's invention of the worker as an identity category to the specific ways that artificial intelligence is now dissolving that category. These chapters may be uncomfortable reading, because they ask you to recognize in yourself the very pathologies they describe. This recognition is the beginning of the cure.

The second movement — Chapters Four through Six — is analytic. It examines the specific psychological mechanisms by which the Identity Crash unfolds: the Worth Paradox that leaves us feeling poorer in a world of unprecedented abundance, the Dopamine Trap that captures our attention in the vacuum left by eroded purpose, and the Human Renaissance that is already beginning in the quiet corners of culture where people are discovering what truly cannot be automated.

The third movement — Chapters Seven through Ten — is constructive. It offers practical architecture for a new kind of life: the Post-Utility Blueprint, specific strategies for navigating the transition, a new map of the professions and roles that will define human contribution in the age of intelligent machines, and a vision of how we might educate the next generation for a world their predecessors did not anticipate.

The Conclusion and Afterword attempt to hold the whole arc together — to say, as clearly and honestly as possible, what I believe the Identity Crash means for the human project, and what we owe each other as we navigate it together.

Finally, the Appendices offer practical tools — including a guided Identity Inventory exercise and an annotated reading list — for those who want to go deeper on specific themes.

The machine has taken the work. What remains is the question of what to do with the life. The answer, this book argues, is everything.

CHAPTER ONE

The Church of the Grind

I. A Question Nobody Thinks to Ask

There is a question so embedded in the operating system of modern life that most people have never once paused to consider it, let alone to seriously question it. It is not a political question or a scientific question or a formal philosophical problem. It is far more intimate than any of those. It is the question that lives in the first conscious moments of every working morning, before the alarm has fully registered, before the coffee has brewed, before the obligations of the day have assembled themselves into their familiar queue.

The question is this: What do I need to do today?

Not "What do I want to do today?" Not "What would genuinely nourish me today?" Not "What would make this a day worth remembering?" But what do I need to do. What is required. What is expected. What will mark this Tuesday as legitimate in the ledger of a productive life well-spent. The default orientation is entirely toward production, toward completion, toward the satisfaction of external demands so thoroughly internalized that they no longer feel external at all.

This orientation is so pervasive, so normalized, so completely integrated into the texture of contemporary existence that questioning it can feel not merely unusual but vaguely heretical. The person who chooses, on a given morning, to sit at their kitchen table and watch the light change for an hour—doing nothing, producing nothing, optimizing nothing—is not merely unproductive by the standards of the Church of the Grind. They are, in some quiet but genuine sense, transgressive. A quiet rebel against a faith so total it has forgotten it is a faith.

This book begins with that transgression. It begins with the insistence that the question "What do I need to do today?" is not the only question available to a human being standing at the beginning of a morning—and that the relentless privileging of that question over all others is, in fact, the source of one of the deepest and most poorly understood psychological crises of the contemporary world. Before we can understand the Identity Crash, we must understand the identity it is crashing. And that identity was built, brick by brick and generation by generation, inside the walls of the Church of the Grind.

II. The Original Human Condition

To understand how we arrived at the Church of the Grind, it is necessary to go back much further than most histories of work typically venture. Not to the Industrial Revolution, and not even to the agricultural settlements of the Fertile Crescent, but to the vast, dimly lit expanse of deep human prehistory—to the world of the hunter-gatherer, which represents not a brief preliminary chapter in human experience, but most of it.

Homo sapiens has existed as a recognizable species for somewhere between two hundred and three hundred thousand years. For ninety-five percent of that span—approximately two hundred and eighty thousand years—we lived in small, mobile bands, subsisting on the plants, animals, and seasonal resources of whatever landscape we inhabited. We did not farm. We did not manufacture. We did not, in any meaningful sense, have careers.

The anthropological evidence regarding the labor requirements of hunter-gatherer life is both robust and, by contemporary standards, genuinely astonishing. Studies of modern hunter-gatherer societies—the !Kung San of the Kalahari, the Hadza of Tanzania, the Aboriginal Australians of the Western Desert—consistently find that the acquisition of sufficient food and resources for daily subsistence requires, on average, between three and five hours of active effort per day. Not eight hours. Not twelve. Three to five.

The Marshall Sahlins essay that gave this finding its most influential formulation, "The Original Affluent Society," published in 1972, described hunter-gatherers not as the desperately impoverished, constantly struggling primitives of popular imagination, but as people who had, in a specific and meaningful sense, solved the problem of material sufficiency with remarkable efficiency. Their wants were modest, their means were adequate to meet those wants, and the result was something that looks, from ten thousand years of civilization, disconcertingly like leisure.

This is not a romanticized fantasy of primitive paradise. Hunter-gatherer life was also characterized by significant physical danger, by the ever-present threat of violence, by infant mortality rates that would horrify any modern parent, and by the absence of the medical, technological, and cultural achievements that make contemporary life genuinely extraordinary in many respects. The point is not that the hunter-gatherer world was better. The point is that it was different, in a specific way that matters enormously for the story this chapter tells: work was instrumental, not constitutive. It was a means to the end of living, not the substance of living itself.

In the hunter-gatherer world, a person's identity was embedded in their kinship network, their relationship to the spiritual forces that governed the natural world, their reputation as a storyteller, a healer, a hunter, a mediator of disputes, an interpreter of dreams. They were not, in any meaningful sense, what they produced. They were who they were in relation to the people and powers around them. Work was something they did. It was not something they were.

III. The Agricultural Bargain

The Agricultural Revolution, which began its slow spread approximately twelve thousand years ago in the arc of land stretching from modern-day Syria to Iran, represents one of the most consequential and, in many ways, most ambivalent transitions in human history. It was not simply a technological advance, though it was certainly that. It was a fundamental reorganization of the relationship between human beings, labor, and time.

The cultivation of crops and the domestication of animals created, for the first time in human history, the sustained possibility of surplus—the production of more food than was immediately needed for subsistence. Surplus made storage, and storage made possible the accumulation of wealth across seasons and years. Accumulation made hierarchy—the emergence of social stratifications based on differential access to stored resources. And hierarchy made possible, for the first time, the organized extraction of labor: the direction of one group of people's productive effort toward the accumulation of another group's wealth.

Jared Diamond, in his provocative 1987 essay "The Worst Mistake in the History of the Human Race," argued that the transition to agriculture represented, for the average human being, a sharp decline in quality of life: longer working hours, worse nutrition (because of dependence on a narrower range of foods), increased susceptibility to epidemic disease (because of living in close proximity to both domesticated animals and large numbers of other humans), and a dramatic increase in social inequality. Diamond's argument remains controversial among archaeologists and anthropologists, but the core of his claim—that the agricultural bargain was a far more complicated transaction than our cultural mythology typically acknowledges—is supported by considerable evidence.

But even the agricultural revolution, for all its transformation of material conditions, did not fully remake human identity in the specific way that concerns us here. The medieval peasant who spent twelve hours a day in the fields did not, by most accounts, experience those twelve hours as the center of his selfhood. His identity was organized around other axes entirely: his place in a divinely ordered cosmos, his membership in a village community, his relationship to the seasonal rhythms of planting and harvest, his obligations to his family and his lord, his standing in the eyes of the God he prayed to every morning and every night.

Work, for the medieval peasant, was the inescapable texture of daily life. It was also, in the Benedictine tradition that shaped much of medieval European culture, a form of prayer—a participation in the divine order of creation, a collaboration with God's ongoing work of sustaining the world. Ora et labora: pray and work. The two were not in tension. They were expressions of the same fundamental orientation toward existence as gift and obligation, received from above and returned through faithful daily effort.

The identity of the pre-industrial laborer was embedded in a web of meaning that extended far beyond the content of the labor itself. The work was hard, often brutal, frequently unjust—but it was not, in the modern sense, existentially defining. It was not who you were. It was what you did to be who you were.

IV. The Industrial Revolution and the Making of the Worker

The decisive rupture—the one that created the specifically modern pathology that the Identity Crash is now forcing us to abandon—was the Industrial Revolution of the eighteenth and nineteenth centuries. And its mechanism was not simply economic, though it was profoundly economic. At its deepest level, it was a revolution in the organization of identity itself.

The factory system that emerged from the textile mills of Lancashire and Yorkshire and the ironworks of the English Midlands did something that no previous form of labor organization had ever done with such thoroughness or such deliberateness: it stripped work of its context. The craftsman of the medieval guild could look at the chair he had spent three days making and say, with genuine pride and a full account of the process: I made that. The farmer of the early modern period could look at the harvest and say: I grew this, from this soil, with these hands, in this season. Even the most exploited agricultural laborer existed within a web of relationships, seasons, and local knowledge that gave the labor a kind of meaning, however attenuated.

The factory worker on the assembly line in 1880 had no such consolation. He tightened the same bolt ten thousand times a day. He had no relationship to the raw materials that entered the factory, no knowledge of the finished product that left it, no contact with the end user whose life his labor was theoretically improving. He was, in the most precise sense, a unit of production: a replaceable, interchangeable component in a system whose purpose was entirely invisible to him. His labor was not a craft. It was not a calling. It was not a participation in any larger meaning. It was a commodity, exchanged for wages at the going market rate.

In response to this profound alienation—this radical disconnection between labor and meaning that the factory system created—a remarkable and, in retrospect, entirely understandable psychological compensation emerged. Western industrial culture began, with increasing fervor and creativity, to moralize work itself. If the content of labor had become meaningless, then the act of laboring—the effort, the endurance, the willingness to submit oneself to the factory's demands day after day—would be elevated into a virtue in its own right. Idleness became not merely impractical but sinful. Busyness became not merely necessary but noble. Overwork became not merely common but admirable.

The intellectual scaffolding for this transformation was provided, most influentially, by the theology of Calvinist Protestantism and its secular descendants. Max Weber's masterwork "The Protestant Ethic and the Spirit of Capitalism," published in 1905, traced with brilliant precision the pathway by which the Calvinist doctrine of predestination—the terrifying belief that God had already determined, before the foundation of the world, which souls would be saved and which damned, and that nothing a person did in this life could alter that determination—produced, paradoxically, an intensification of worldly labor rather than a relaxation into fatalism.

The logic was circuitous but psychologically powerful: since worldly success could not produce salvation, but God would allow his elect to prosper in worldly affairs, evidence of worldly prosperity could serve as a kind of indirect, probabilistic evidence of election. The successful merchant, the diligent laborer, the farmer who turned his land to maximum account was not thereby guaranteed a place among the saved—but the very fact of his success suggested that God had not abandoned him.

Anxiety about salvation was managed through productive effort, and productive effort was rewarded with prosperity, and prosperity was taken as provisional evidence of divine favor. The feedback loop was self-reinforcing, addictive, and, over time, entirely self-sustaining even after the explicitly religious motivation had faded.

Within a few generations, the idea that a person's worth was equivalent to their productive output had become so deeply embedded in Western consciousness that it no longer required theological justification. It had become, in the fullest sense, secular gospel. The work ethic had been successfully decoupled from the religious framework that gave it birth and transplanted into the soil of industrial capitalism, where it flourished with extraordinary vigor. The Church of the Grind had been founded. And its congregation, over the next two centuries, would grow to encompass the entirety of the modern world.

V. The Twentieth Century: When Work Became the Self

If the Industrial Revolution created the conditions for the Church of the Grind, the twentieth century built its cathedral. The successive developments of the century—scientific management, the corporate organization, the consumer economy, the knowledge economy, and the digital revolution—each added new spires, new buttresses, and new stained glass to the edifice of work-as-identity, until by the century's end it had achieved an architectural grandeur that made it impossible to see from the outside.

Frederick Winslow Taylor's "Principles of Scientific Management," published in 1911, established the conceptual framework that would govern industrial organization for decades: the systematic decomposition of any productive task into its smallest components, the measurement of each component to determine its optimal execution time, and the redesign of work processes to eliminate all inefficiency. Taylor's method was not merely an engineering protocol. It was an ontological claim: that human beings, in their working capacity, were machines whose performance could be optimized through the application of scientific principles.

Taylorism, as it came to be known, was enormously successful on its own terms. Its application to industrial production generated dramatic increases in output and corresponding reductions in unit labor cost. It also, over time, generated something else: a workforce that had been trained, both practically and psychologically, to understand their own value in purely quantitative, output-oriented terms. You were worth what you produced per hour. Your identity was your productivity. The two had become, in the Taylorist imagination, not merely correlated but definitionally equivalent.

The mid-century corporation took this individual equation and scaled it to the level of an entire social world. The great American corporations of the 1950s and 60s—IBM, General Motors, AT&T, Standard Oil—were, in the sociological analysis of William Whyte and C. Wright Mills, total institutions: organizations that provided not merely employment but the full architecture of a social existence. Company towns. Company health care. Company pension plans. Company social clubs. Company identity. The "organization man" whom Whyte described in his 1956 masterpiece of the same name had traded personal autonomy for institutional belonging, individual identity for corporate identity, and had done so with a willingness that bordered on gratitude.

The corporate organization man—and he was, at this stage of history, exclusively a man—knew precisely who he was because he knew precisely where he worked and what rank he occupied within the organizational hierarchy. His identity was institutional. It was stable, legible, and socially recognized. "I work for IBM" was not merely an employment status. It was a full account of oneself: one's values, one's aspirations, one's place in the social order, one's trajectory through life.

The women's liberation movement of the 1960s and 70s challenged this arrangement in ways that were both necessary and historically ambivalent. The critique of the domestic sphere as a site of women's confinement and diminishment was accurate, urgent, and politically essential. The demand for women's equal access to professional life was morally correct and transformative. But the cultural logic of the liberation—the implicit equation of freedom with professional participation, of self-realization with career achievement—extended the reach of the Church of the Grind rather than challenging its foundations. By the 1980s, the promise of liberation had been absorbed into the ideology of productive identity: now everyone—not just men—could define themselves through their work. The congregation had doubled. The church had not changed.

VI. The Knowledge Economy and the Colonization of the Mind

The decisive final development in the construction of the Church of the Grind was the emergence of the knowledge economy in the final decades of the twentieth century. This development is the one most directly relevant to the Identity Crash, because it is the one that created the specific form of work-as-identity that is now most thoroughly threatened by artificial intelligence.

The industrial economy had colonized the body: it demanded physical labor, measured physical output, and reduced human workers to the productive capacity of their muscles and endurance. The knowledge economy went further. It colonized the mind. It transformed cognitive capacity—intelligence, expertise, analytical skill, creative judgment—from a personal attribute that one happened to bring to one's work into the primary commodity that one's professional existence consisted in offering to the market.

The lawyer, the consultant, the software engineer, the financial analyst, the management strategist, the academic researcher—these were not merely people who worked with their minds rather than their hands. They were people whose professional existence was constituted by the market value of their mental content. Their knowledge, their judgment, their trained intelligence was not an instrument they used in their work. It was the work. They were not merely producers of cognitive outputs. In a very real and deeply felt sense, they were the outputs.

This fusion of personal identity with cognitive product is what makes the arrival of artificial general cognitive capability so uniquely devastating to the modern professional class. When the factory worker's job was automated, the threat was economic: a loss of income, a need to retrain, a disruption of a specific labor market. The identity damage was real but indirect—mediated by the economic consequences of displacement. When the knowledge worker's cognitive capacity is matched or exceeded by a machine, the threat is immediate and personal. It is not merely that their job is at risk. It is that the specific thing they have spent years developing and have most deeply understood themselves to be—the expert, the specialist, the uniquely capable analyst or strategist or creator—has been replicated by a system with no such investment, no such struggle, and no such claim to unique human distinction.

The Identity Crash is, in this sense, the knowledge economy's specific existential crisis. It is the moment when the cognitive outputs that the knowledge economy elevated to the status of personal identity are revealed to be commodities rather than essences. When the ten-thousand hours of mastery that the knowledge worker was told would make them irreplaceable turn out to have made them, at most, a high-quality approximation of something a machine can now approximate more efficiently.

VII. The Hustle Gospel: Faith at its Most Fervent

By the early decades of the twenty-first century, the Church of the Grind had reached the apex of its influence. Silicon Valley and its global imitators produced a new theology of work that was, in its fervor and its demands, more extreme than anything the Protestant work ethic or scientific management had ever required. This theology went by various names—the hustle culture, the startup mentality, the growth mindset—but its core doctrines were consistent across all its variations.

The first doctrine was total commitment: the idea that genuine dedication to one's work required not merely diligence during working hours but the subordination of every other dimension of life—health, relationships, rest, play, contemplation, even sleep—to the demands of professional achievement. "Sleep is for the weak." "Rest when you're dead." "If you're not working on your dream, someone else is working on theirs." These aphorisms, repeated across a thousand motivational Instagram posts and LinkedIn thought-leadership pieces, were not merely inspirational rhetoric. They were doctrinal statements: explicit formulations of the belief that a person's entire existence should be organized around the maximization of professional output.

The second doctrine was perpetual self-optimization: the idea that the primary obligation of a person who wished to thrive in the knowledge economy was the continuous, systematic improvement of their human capital—their skills, their networks, their personal brand, their emotional intelligence, their physical health (insofar as it served professional performance), their mental agility. The self-optimization industry—the books, the podcasts, the apps, the courses, the coaching programs—became one of the fastest-growing sectors of the consumer economy, generating tens of billions of dollars annually from people who were purchasing access to frameworks for becoming more efficiently useful to the market.

The third doctrine, and the most insidious, was the equation of passion with work. The injunction to "find your passion" and "do what you love" sounds, on its surface, like an encouragement of authentic self-expression. In the context of the Church of the Grind, it functions as something more demanding: the instruction to ensure that your deepest enthusiasms, your most genuine interests, your most authentic sources of pleasure are all directed toward economically productive ends. Find your passion—and monetize it. Love what you do—and make sure it generates a return. The interior life is not to be protected from the market's demands. It is to be offered to the market as its most valuable raw material.

Hustle culture was, and remains, disproportionately powerful in its hold over the aspirational young. For the generation that came of age in the first two decades of the twenty-first century—the millennials and the early cohort of Generation Z who graduated into the shadow of the 2008 financial crisis, entered a labor market of radical precarity, and watched the institutional structures of stable professional identity that had anchored their parents' lives dissolve in real time—the hustle gospel offered something that is irresistible to people in states of profound uncertainty: clarity. You know who you are because you know what you are building. You know what your life is for because you have a roadmap, a metrics dashboard, and a daily schedule optimized for maximum output.

The fact that this clarity was, in retrospect, purchased at an enormous psychological cost—the epidemic rates of anxiety, depression, and burnout that precisely characterize the demographic most thoroughly colonized by hustle culture—did not immediately undermine its appeal. The Church of the Grind, like all powerful ideological systems, had explanations ready for its failures. Burnout was evidence of insufficient resilience. Depression was a productivity problem to be solved with therapy, medication, and better time management. Exhaustion was a signal to optimize one's recovery protocols.

The one thing the Church of the Grind could not do, within its own framework, was acknowledge that the framework itself was the problem. That the relentless equation of selfhood with productive utility was not merely unsustainable but fundamentally false—a category error of the most profound kind, mistaking a historically contingent economic arrangement for a permanent and necessary feature of what it means to be a person.

VIII. The Walls Begin to Shake

The first significant tremors in the walls of the Church of the Grind did not come from artificial intelligence. They came from the generation that had been most thoroughly indoctrinated in its doctrines and had most completely organized their lives around its demands—and had found, in the lived experience of that organization, that the promised payoffs were not materializing.

The phenomenon that journalists began describing in the early 2020s under the heading of "the Great Resignation" was not, despite the name, primarily a story about people quitting jobs. It was a story about people leaving the Church of the Grind—or attempting to leave it. The millions of workers who voluntarily departed their positions in the period following the COVID-19 pandemic were, in many cases, not leaving work for idleness. They were leaving the specific form of work—the work organized entirely around institutional productivity, professional identity, and the subordination of everything else to career achievement—in search of something that had no agreed-upon name but that many of them described, in interviews and surveys, in terms of meaning, presence, and the simple experience of being alive for their own lives rather than for their employer's quarterly returns.

The pandemic itself had been, for many people, an involuntary experiment in living without the Church of the Grind—or at least without its most demanding rituals. The enforced removal from the office, the disruption of the daily commute and the nine-to-five structure, the sudden proximity to family members and domestic life, the confrontation with illness and mortality that the pandemic imposed on even its most fortunate observers—all of this had, for many people, the effect of a sudden clearing. The noise of the Grind had momentarily subsided, and in the resulting quiet, people had discovered something that surprised them: that the aspects of their lives they most valued had little to do with their professional productivity.

These cultural tremors preceded the arrival of artificial intelligence as a mass phenomenon. But they created the psychological conditions in which the Identity Crash, when it came, would land with force. A significant cohort of the professional class had already begun to suspect that the Church of the Grind was asking more than it could deliver. The arrival of AI—which did not merely challenge the Church's demands but delegitimized its entire ontological framework by demonstrating that cognitive productivity, the Church's most sacred offering, was not exclusively human—would confirm and accelerate those suspicions with a velocity that the ordinary pace of cultural change could not have produced.

The crash, in other words, was already underway before the machines arrived. The machines merely—and decisively—completed it.

IX. The Anatomy of a Collapsing Faith

What does it feel like when the central organizing faith of a life begins to lose its power to compel? The phenomenology of the Identity Crash—the lived experience of the person who has built their entire sense of self on the foundation of professional identity and is now watching that foundation erode—is worth examining with some care, because it is so frequently misdiagnosed by both its sufferers and by those attempting to help them.

It does not, typically, feel like a sudden loss of faith. It feels, initially, more like a growing unease. A slight but persistent dissonance between the official narrative of one's professional life—the accomplished resume, the impressive title, the track record of delivered results—and the private experience of performing that narrative. The sense that the activities one is being paid to perform are becoming progressively less connected to anything that feels genuinely real, genuinely challenging, or genuinely significant.

This unease is easy to dismiss or rationalize in its initial stages. Everyone has periods of disengagement. Everyone goes through professional seasons of reduced enthusiasm. The standard prescription—a vacation, a new project, a promotion, a lateral move to a more interesting team—addresses the surface symptoms while leaving the underlying condition entirely untouched. The person returns from their vacation, takes on their new project, and finds, after a few weeks, that the unease has returned. Slightly deeper this time. Slightly harder to dismiss.

As the unease deepens, it typically begins to produce the specific psychological symptoms associated with what clinicians call existential crisis: a loss of the sense of purpose and direction that had previously organized one's experience of time; a growing difficulty finding genuine motivation for activities that once engaged genuine enthusiasm; a pervasive sense of fraudulence, of performing a role whose script has become simultaneously too familiar and incomprehensible; and, underlying all of these, a question that surfaces in the small hours of the morning with increasing insistence: If this is not the point, then what is?

This question—if this is not the point, then what is?—is the crack in the wall of the Church of the Grind through which the light of the Human Renaissance can eventually enter. It is not, in the first instance, a comfortable question. It is frightening, destabilizing, and deeply lonely, because it is a question that the surrounding culture—still thoroughly committed to the gospel of productive identity—is not equipped to take seriously. The person who raises it is often told, with genuine kindness and genuine misunderstanding, to find a new job, take up a hobby, reconnect with their passion, or be grateful for what they have.

None of these responses addresses the question because none of them challenges the premise that generated it. The premise is the one we began this chapter with: that the right question for a human being to ask at the beginning of a morning is "What do I need to do today?" The right response to the Identity Crash is not to find a better answer to that question. It is to learn to ask a different question entirely.

X. Toward a Different Question

The different question is one that human beings have been asking, in one form or another, for as long as consciousness has existed. It is the question that the great philosophical and spiritual traditions of every culture have, in their several ways, centrally addressed. It is the question that the Church of the Grind, in its two centuries of cultural dominance, has done everything in its power to obscure, marginalize, and replace with more productive inquiries.

The question is not "What do I need to do today?" but "What kind of person do I want to be?" Not "What am I worth to the market?" but "What is a human life for?" Not "How can I be more productive?" but "How can I be more fully alive?"

These questions cannot be answered by an optimization algorithm, however sophisticated. They cannot be resolved by the accumulation of credentials, the achievement of professional milestones, or the satisfaction of a performance review. They are, by their nature, the questions that belong to the domain of being rather than doing—the domain that artificial intelligence, for all its extraordinary capabilities, cannot enter, because being is precisely what AI does not do.

The Identity Crash, painful as it is, is in this sense a gift—though a gift of the kind that arrives wrapped in crisis rather than in ribbon. It is the moment when the questions that the Church of the Grind has been suppressing for two hundred years are finally too insistent to ignore. When the scaffolding of productive identity has been shaken sufficiently that the person standing within it can, for the first time, see it for what it is: a scaffolding, not a foundation. A historically contingent arrangement of economic incentives and cultural values, not the permanent and necessary structure of a human life.

The chapters that follow are an attempt to help the reader inhabit the time after the scaffolding comes down. To navigate the disorientation, resist the traps, recover what was lost beneath the construction, and build—slowly, deliberately, and with full awareness of the difficulty of the project—a form of identity that is not contingent on the market's assessment of one's cognitive productivity. An identity that is grounded, instead, in the things that make human existence genuinely and irreducibly valuable: embodiment, relationship, creative irrationality, shared suffering, and the quiet, durable, algorithm-proof act of being genuinely, completely, and irreversibly alive.

The Grind is over. The life is about to begin.

CHAPTER TWO

THE EFFICIENCY WALL

✦ ✦ ✦

I. THE COMFORTABLE MISUNDERSTANDING

Every era constructs its own version of the future, and every version is wrong in precisely the same way: it imagines the future as a linear extension of the present. The technologies change: the social arrangements shift; the specific content of daily life evolves beyond recognition. But the fundamental hierarchy — the arrangement of who oversees what, of which entities serve which purposes, of what belongs to humans and what belongs to machines — remains, in the imagination of each era, stable. More of the same. Faster, bigger, more powerful — but recognizably continuous with what came before.

This is the lens through which the twentieth century imagined artificial intelligence. Even the most visionary thinkers of the computer age, with a handful of prescient exceptions, understood the emerging technology through the framework of the tool: something picked up when needed and set down when done. The computer was a calculator. A filing cabinet. A communication system. An extraordinarily powerful instrument, certainly — but an instrument, nonetheless. Something that extended human capacity without replacing human agency. Something that served human purposes rather than defining them.

The assumption was not merely comforting. It was, for most of computing history, accurate. The first generation of computers — the ENIAC, the UNIVAC, the early IBM mainframes — were, in the most literal sense, enormously expensive, room-sized adding machines. They performed arithmetic operations at speeds no human could approach. They stored and retrieved data with perfect fidelity. But they were entirely dependent on human beings for every meaningful dimension of their operation: for the definition of problems, the structuring of inputs, the interpretation of outputs, and the determination of what any of it meant or should be used for.

Even as the power of computing systems grew exponentially across the following decades — through the transistor revolution, through integrated circuits, through the microprocessor, through the personal computing explosion of the 1980s and the internet revolution of the 1990s — this fundamental dependency remained intact. Computers were faster, smaller, cheaper, more pervasive, and vastly more capable than their predecessors. But they remained, in the architecturally decisive sense, servants. Extraordinarily capable servants, but servants. The hierarchy was intact. The human was still in charge.

This is the misunderstanding that defined an era. Not a foolish misunderstanding — it was an honest extrapolation from genuinely accurate observations about the nature of computing at every previous stage of its development. But it created a mental model that left the professional class entirely unprepared for the specific nature of the disruption that was approaching. They were expecting a better hammer. They received something that had learned to swing.

II. What the Efficiency Wall Actually Is

The term "Efficiency Wall" is used in this book to describe something specific, and it is worth being precise about what that something is — because the precision matters for understanding both the nature of the crisis it describes and the nature of the response it requires.

The Efficiency Wall is not the wall above which machines cannot rise. That is the wall we imagined — the theoretical ceiling of machine capability, perpetually receding before advancing technology but always present, always marking the boundary beyond which human uniqueness was safe. The history of artificial intelligence is, in one sense, simply the history of that imagined wall moving: from arithmetic to chess, from chess to language translation, from translation to medical diagnosis, from diagnosis to creative writing, from creative writing to strategic planning. Every time the wall was reached, it turned out not to be a wall at all, but merely a temporary horizon that dissolved as the technology advanced.

The Efficiency Wall, as used here, is the wall behind us. It is not the ceiling that machines cannot breach; it is the threshold we have already crossed. The point of no return. The boundary between a world in which human cognitive labor had market value primarily because it was the only available source of certain kinds of cognitive output, and a world in which that is no longer true. A world in which the availability of machine-generated cognitive output at near-zero marginal cost has permanently transformed the economics of human intellectual labor in ways that cannot be reversed by any amount of training, retraining, or professional development.

To understand what crossing this wall means — and why it is so much more disorienting than any previous technological transition — it is necessary to examine its three principal components in some detail. The Speed Gap. The Death of the Ten-Thousand-Hour Rule. The Perfection Paradox. Each of these is a distinct dimension of the same underlying transformation, and together they constitute a complete account of why the Efficiency Wall is not merely an economic disruption but an identity crisis.

III. The Speed Gap: A Difference of Kind, Not Degree

Begin with a fact that is simultaneously well-known and rarely genuinely absorbed: human neurons transmit electrochemical signals at a maximum velocity of approximately 120 meters per second. This is the biological speed limit of human thought. It is constrained by the physical properties of axonal membranes, myelin sheaths, the chemistry of synaptic transmission, and the thermodynamic limits of biological computation. It is not a performance metric that can be improved through training, supplementation, sleep optimization, or any currently conceivable medical intervention. It is the speed at which carbon-based nervous systems of our architectural type can operate. It is what we are.

The electronic circuits through which modern AI systems perform their computations transmit signals at approximately two-thirds the speed of light in a vacuum — 200,000 kilometers per second, or approximately 450 million miles per hour. The difference between 120 meters per second and 200,000,000 meters per second is not a difference of degree. It is a difference of kind. It is six orders of magnitude: a factor of 1.6 million. If human neural transmission were a person walking at average pace, electronic signal transmission would be a beam of light.

For most of computing history, this raw speed advantage was irrelevant to questions of cognitive competition between humans and machines, because raw processing speed without intelligent direction is merely fast noise. A computer that can perform arithmetic operations a million times faster than a human being is not thereby better at understanding what arithmetic problems are worth solving, what the results mean, or how they should be used. The speed was present; the intelligence to direct it was not. And the missing intelligence was, for decades, the only thing that mattered.

What the successive waves of machine learning research — and particularly the transformer architecture that underlies the most capable large language models — have done is close the gap between raw processing speed and directed cognitive capability. Not eliminate it. Not make machine intelligence identical to human intelligence, or even equivalent to it in all the ways that matter. But close it sufficiently, in sufficiently many domains, that the speed advantage has begun to translate into a genuine cognitive advantage in the specific tasks that most knowledge work consists of.

Consider what this means in practice. A skilled financial analyst, working intensively, might process and synthesize a complex set of quarterly reports in eight to twelve hours. A well-trained AI system processes the same material in seconds — not, but. The same is true for legal document review, medical literature synthesis, code debugging, market research, competitive analysis, and a hundred other specific cognitive tasks that constitute the daily substance of knowledge work. The human expert brings irreplaceable things to these tasks: contextual judgment, ethical discernment, creative insight, the ability to notice what the data is failing to say. But in the specific dimension of information processing speed, the comparison is not competitive. It is not even close.

The Speed Gap matters not only as an economic reality but as a psychological one. One of the most consistent findings in the psychology of self-efficacy — the belief in one's own capacity to accomplish valued goals — is that it is grounded in comparison: we understand ourselves as capable or incapable, fast or slow, skilled, or unskilled, primarily in relation to other agents performing the same tasks. When the only available comparison was other human beings, human cognitive speed was simply a distribution: some people were faster, some slower, all within the same order of magnitude. The fastest human analyst was twice as fast as the slowest. The comparison was legible, comprehensible, and psychologically manageable.

The Speed Gap introduced by AI comparison is not legible in the same way. It exceeds the intuitive grasp of human magnitude perception. The knowledge worker who discovers that a task they spent a full day completing can be performed by a machine in thirty seconds is not experiencing a difference they can easily integrate into a revised self-assessment. They are experiencing something more like an ontological rupture: a sudden, visceral revelation that the dimension along which they have organized their professional identity — their trained capacity to process and synthesize information — is operating at a scale that makes direct comparison not merely unflattering but almost meaningless.

IV. The Death of the Ten-Thousand-Hour Rule

In 2008, Malcolm Gladwell published Outliers, and with it brought to mass cultural attention a finding from the expertise research of psychologist Anders Ericsson that would spend the following decade reshaping how millions of people thought about talent, achievement, and the relationship between effort and mastery. The finding, which Gladwell condensed into what became known as the "ten-thousand-hour rule," was this: that world-class expertise in any complex domain — chess, music, surgery, athletic performance, software engineering — requires approximately ten thousand hours of deliberate, focused, feedback-rich practice to achieve.

The cultural resonance of this finding was immediate and enormous, and not difficult to understand. In a meritocratic cultural context that was simultaneously committed to the ideology of effort-as-destiny and anxious about the role of innate talent in determining outcomes, the ten-thousand-hour rule offered a profoundly democratizing reassurance: expertise is not the exclusive province of the gifted. It is the earned achievement of the diligent. Anyone, with sufficient time and deliberate effort, can become genuinely excellent at anything they choose to master. The investment required is large. The payoff is real. The path is available to all who are willing to walk it.

This narrative was, and remains, substantially accurate as a description of how human expertise develops. Ericsson's research on deliberate practice is genuinely rigorous, genuinely illuminating, and genuinely important for anyone interested in the cultivation of human skill. The ten-thousand-hour rule as a prescription for developing human mastery is not wrong. What it could not anticipate — because nothing in its historical context suggested the need to anticipate it — was the world in which the primary competitive context for human expertise would no longer be other human experts.

Large language models and other AI systems do not develop expertise through deliberate practice. They do not spend ten thousand hours — or any hours — struggling with feedback, refining their performance against expert standards, building the tacit knowledge that Ericsson's research identified as the core product of deliberate practice. They acquire something that functions, in many practical respects, like expertise through a fundamentally different process: the statistical ingestion and pattern-extraction of vast quantities of text, code, data, and other structured information produced by human experts over the course of their ten-thousand-hour journeys.

To be more precise: a large language model trained on the collected textual output of human knowledge — the papers, the case studies, the code repositories, the clinical notes, the legal briefs, the analytical reports, the design specifications — does not learn what an individual expert learned through their ten thousand hours. It learns the patterns that the collective output of millions of experts, each with their own ten thousand hours, have deposited in the textual record of human civilization. Its "training" ingests not the equivalent of one expert's decade of deliberate practice, but something closer to the aggregate of all such decades that have been legibly expressed.

The implications of this for the economics of human expertise are stark and, for many professionals, genuinely difficult to accept. The ten thousand hours you invested in becoming an expert financial analyst, contract lawyer, diagnostic radiologist, or software architect represent a genuine and extraordinary human achievement. The knowledge and judgment you developed through that investment are real. They are not rendered worthless by the existence of AI systems capable of performing many of the same tasks. But they have been rendered significantly less scarce — and scarcity, in a market economy, is the primary determinant of price.

When the outputs of ten thousand hours of human expertise can be approximated, for many specific task types, by a system that required no such investment and can be replicated at near-zero marginal cost, the market premium attached to the possession of that expertise contracts sharply. Not to zero — there remain dimensions of human expertise that AI approximation cannot yet reach, and there likely always will be. But to a level that is structurally incompatible with the economic arrangements and professional identities built on the assumption that rare, hard-won human expertise is the primary source of knowledge-economy value.

The death of the ten-thousand-hour rule as an economic guarantee is not the death of deliberate practice as a human value. The capacity to develop mastery through sustained, disciplined engagement remains one of the most deeply meaningful activities available to a human being — not because it produces market-valuable expertise, but because the process of developing mastery is itself transformative. It builds character, depth, attentional capacity, and the specific kind of pride that comes from having genuinely earned something difficult. These are values that persist regardless of whether the market rewards them. Understanding this distinction — between the market value of expertise and the human value of the journey toward mastery — is one of the central cognitive tasks of navigating the post-Efficiency Wall world.

V. The Perfection Paradox: When Flawlessness Becomes a Liability

The third component of the Efficiency Wall is the most counterintuitive, and the one most pregnant with unexpected possibility. It is what this chapter calls the Perfection Paradox: the phenomenon by which the proliferation of algorithmically perfect cognitive outputs produces, paradoxically, an increase in the value of human imperfection.

To understand the Perfection Paradox, it helps to think about what has happened in another domain where technological progress produced a similar dynamic — one that is far enough in the past to be visible clearly, without the distorting closeness of the current crisis. Consider the history of photographic portraiture.

Before the invention of photography in the mid-nineteenth century, a painted portrait was the only way to create a durable visual record of a person's appearance. Portraiture was a highly skilled craft, requiring years of training and practice, and the cost of commissioning a portrait placed it firmly beyond the reach of most people. The portrait artist occupied a position of genuine scarcity and genuine social prestige: they possessed a capability that was rare, valuable, and in demand.

The arrival of photography changed this completely and rapidly. Within a few decades of the daguerreotype's introduction, photographic portraiture had made it possible for any person to obtain an accurate visual record of their own face at a fraction of the cost of a painted portrait. The market for traditional portraiture collapsed. Many portrait painters found themselves economically displaced by a technology that could produce, for practical purposes, a more accurate representation of a subject's physical appearance in seconds rather than hours.

And yet — this is the crucial observation — painted portraiture did not disappear. It survived, and over the following century it thrived, not by competing with photography on photography's terms (accuracy, speed, cost) but by retreating to the dimensions of value that photography could not replicate: the artist's interpretive vision, the emotional weight of a hand-rendered surface, the visible record of the painter's engagement with the subject, the irreducible presence of human attention that a painted portrait embodies and that a photograph, however technically perfect, does not.

The market for painted portraiture did not recover its pre-photographic scale. But what remained of it commanded, and continues to command, prices that no photograph — however technically brilliant — approaches. Not because painted portraits are more accurate. Precisely because they are less accurate. Because they are marked by the choices, the interpretations, and the inevitable imperfections of a human maker whose engagement with the subject produced something that cannot be replicated by any mechanical process, however sophisticated.

This dynamic — technological perfection creating a premium for human imperfection — is now being replicated across the entirety of knowledge work with a speed and comprehensiveness that the portrait painter's experience could not have prepared us for. As AI systems become capable of producing legal briefs, financial analyses, diagnostic reports, design specifications, and strategic plans that are faster, more consistent, and free of the specific types of error to which human cognition is prone, the market value of these outputs as commodities contracts sharply. Simultaneously, the value of certain things that AI systems cannot provide — the judgment that goes beyond the data, the wisdom that knows when the technically correct answer is the wrong one, the insight that emerges from lived experience rather than statistical pattern-extraction — increases correspondingly.

The Perfection Paradox tells us something important and hopeful about the post-Efficiency Wall world: it is not a world in which human contribution has no value. It is a world in which the wrong kinds of human contribution — the kinds that were always, at their core, mere approximations of what a sufficiently powerful computing system could do — have lost their scarcity premium, while the right kinds — the kinds that are irreducibly human, irreducibly embodied, irreducibly grounded in the specific experience of being a conscious creature in a physical world — have become correspondingly more valuable.

Logic is now a commodity. Intuition is the new gold. Not the intuition of guesswork or wishful thinking, but the deep, experience-grounded, embodied intelligence that knows what the numbers are failing to say — that can read a room, hold a contradiction, feel the weight of a decision's human consequences, and bring to a situation the irreplaceable perspective of someone who has lived, suffered, chosen, and learned.

VI. The Domains AI Cannot Enter

The Efficiency Wall does not mark the boundary of all human value. It marks the boundary of a specific kind of human value: the market premium attached to cognitive performance in domains where AI systems can now match or exceed human capability at near-zero marginal cost. Beyond that boundary — or rather, beneath it, in the geological sense of something foundational that was always present beneath the surface of the knowledge economy's cultural geology — lie domains of human capability that are not merely currently beyond AI reach but are structurally, architecturally, and perhaps permanently so.

The first of these domains is genuine embodied intelligence — the form of knowing that is inseparable from having a body that interacts with the physical world through sensation, effort, and consequence. A master surgeon's hands know things that cannot be encoded in language. A skilled carpenter's fingers understand wood grain in ways that no amount of visual data can capture. A dancer's body knows rhythm and space through years of proprioceptive experience that leaves traces not in memory but in muscle, tendon, and the neural pathways that connect movement to intention. This is not cognitive knowledge that happens to be stored in a biological system. It is knowledge of a fundamentally different type: tacit, embodied, and entirely dependent on the physical relationship between a nervous system and the material world it inhabits.

AI systems, however sophisticated their processing of information about physical experience, have no physical experience. They can describe embodied intelligence in extraordinary detail. They can analyze its products, predict its outputs, and generate representations of its processes that are accurate in every measurable respect. But they cannot have it. The knowledge is not in the description. It is in the doing, and the doing requires a body that can feel the consequences of its own actions.

The second domain is genuine moral reasoning — not the application of ethical frameworks to abstract cases, but the lived, agonized, consequential navigation of real situations in which multiple valid values conflict, in which the right answer is not obvious and may not exist, and in which the decision-maker's own character — their history of choices, their experience of moral failure, their hard-won understanding of what genuinely matters — is inseparable from the quality of the judgment they exercise. AI systems can process ethical frameworks with impressive sophistication. But they cannot have moral experience — cannot have made choices they regret, cannot have encountered situations that revealed the limits of their previous understanding, cannot have grown, in the specific sense of having been changed by the encounter with genuine moral difficulty.

The third domain is genuine creative disruption — the capacity to produce work that is not merely novel within existing patterns but that challenges, transforms, or transcends the patterns themselves. AI systems are extraordinary generators of pattern-consistent novelty: they can produce, within any established aesthetic, cognitive, or stylistic framework, variations that are creative by any reasonable measure of that term. What they cannot do, given their current architecture, is genuinely depart from the patterns of their training — cannot have the experience of seeing something that the data doesn't contain, of trusting an intuition that the available evidence contradicts, of making the kind of irrational choice that occasionally, in retrospect, reveals itself as the founding act of a new framework.

These three domains — embodied intelligence, genuine moral reasoning, and creative disruption — are not consolation prizes for the cognitively displaced. They are the domains where the most important human contributions to the world have always been made. They are the domains that the Church of the Grind systematically undervalued because they are difficult to measure, difficult to manage, and difficult to integrate into a productivity framework built around the quantification of output. The Efficiency Wall, in forcing us to relocate the center of gravity of human professional value, is also forcing us to finally take seriously the things that were most worth taking seriously all along.

VII. The Psychological Topography of the Wall

Understanding the Efficiency Wall as an intellectual proposition is one thing. Living through the experience of running into it discovering, during one's actual professional life, that a capability you have spent years developing and have organized your identity around is now approximable by a machine — is something else entirely. The psychological experience of the Efficiency Wall deserves its own examination because it is far more complex, far more disorienting, and far more varied across different individuals and contexts than the economic analysis alone would suggest.

For some people, the first encounter with the Efficiency Wall is sudden and unmistakable: a specific moment in which an AI system produces an output — a legal analysis, a piece of code, a design solution, a written report — that is not merely adequate but genuinely impressive. Impressive in a way that triggers a visceral, not merely intellectual, recognition of what is happening. The stomach drops. The familiar professional confidence falters. The question — previously theoretical, suddenly personal — surfaces with force: What, exactly, am I bringing to this that the machine cannot?

For others, the encounter is gradual: a slow accumulation of small recognitions, each individually deniable, that together produce a mounting conviction that the professional landscape is shifting beneath one's feet. The reports take less time to review because the AI first pass is consistently good. The junior staff are producing more sophisticated analysis than their experience would previously have permitted, because they have learned to direct AI systems effectively. The meetings that once required your specific expertise now require only the ability to ask the right questions of a system that has ingested your expertise and everyone else's.

In both cases, the psychological response is shaped by the degree to which professional identity — the sense of self organized around one's cognitive contribution to one's field — is fused with the specific capabilities that the Efficiency Wall is calling into question. For the person, whose professional identity is loosely held — who values their work but does not define themselves by it — the encounter with the Efficiency Wall may be primarily an economic concern, practically demanding but not existentially destabilizing. For the person whose entire self-concept is organized around their professional expertise, the encounter is more like a bereavement: a loss that requires genuine grieving before any genuine adaptation becomes possible.

This is not metaphorical language. The research on the psychology of identity threat — specifically, on the experience of threats to highly central, highly valued components of the self-concept — consistently finds that such threats activate psychological responses that are structurally similar to the responses activated by bereavement and other forms of significant loss. The initial response is typically denial: a search for reasons why the threat is overstated, why the specific capabilities in question are more robust than the disruptive technology suggests, why one's particular version of expertise is protected by dimensions that the general analysis misses. Denial is adaptive in the short term. It preserves functioning while the psyche assembles the resources needed for genuine reckoning. But it is only sustainable until the evidence becomes too comprehensive to explain away.

What follows denial, in the most common pattern, is a period of active mourning: an emotionally charged engagement with the reality of what has been lost, or is being lost, that is painful and disorienting but necessary for genuine adaptation. This is the phase in which the specific content of the grief becomes available for examination: not just the loss of economic security, but the loss of the specific form of professional identity that the Efficiency Wall has called into question. The loss of the sense of being uniquely capable, uniquely trained, uniquely positioned to do something that genuinely needed doing and that only someone with your preparation could do.

And beyond mourning, for those who move through it rather than defending against it, lies something that is genuinely difficult to predict from within the crisis: a form of clarity. A recognition, often arriving with an unexpected quality of relief, that the self that was organized around professional cognitive performance was never the whole self — was never, in fact, the most interesting or most valuable self-available. That the capabilities which were lost to the Efficiency Wall were real and genuine achievements, but they were achievements in the service of a market rather than achievements of the person. And that the person, without those market-validated achievements, remains — is, for the first time in a long time, simply and fully there.

VIII. The Human Premium: What Markets Will Pay For Next

Economics, for all the abstractions of its theoretical frameworks, is a record of what human beings collectively decide to value. The price system is not a neutral mirror of some pre-existing natural order; it is a social construction that reflects, imperfectly and with significant lag, the actual preferences and beliefs of the people who participate in it. And those preferences and beliefs change — sometimes gradually, as cultural values shift over decades, and sometimes with startling speed, when the arrival of a genuinely transformative technology reshuffles the deck of scarcity and abundance in ways that the previous price system could not have anticipated.

The Efficiency Wall is exactly such a transformative technology, and it is in the process of reshuffling the deck in ways that are already visible in nascent form and will become dramatically more pronounced over the coming decade. The reshuffling has a clear directional logic, even if its specific manifestations are difficult to predict in detail: it is creating abundance in the domains where AI performs well and scarcity — genuine, economically significant scarcity — in the domains where it does not.

The emerging Human Premium — the market value attached to capabilities and qualities that are specifically, irreducibly human — is already visible across multiple sectors of the economy, though it is not yet widely recognized as such. The premium commanded by human-created art over algorithmically generated art is not merely a collector's preference for provenance. It is a genuine market signal: that human creative work carries a value that derives not only from its aesthetic qualities but from its status as the product of a human mind, with all the irreducible complexity, vulnerability, and specificity that such a provenance implies.

The premium commanded by human therapeutic relationships over AI-assisted mental health interventions reflects a similar logic: that the value of being genuinely heard, genuinely understood, and genuinely accompanied through difficulty by another human being who has their own experience of difficulty is not reducible to the informational content of what the therapist says. It is grounded in the ontological fact of shared humanity — in the specific form of recognition that is only available from another creature who faces the same fundamental existential conditions.

The premium commanded by hand-crafted objects, locally sourced food, live musical performance, and face-to-face education reflects, in each case, the same underlying dynamic: a market recognition that the human presence in these activities — the visible evidence of human attention, human effort, human care, and human imperfection — constitutes a genuine form of value that is not replicable by automated production, however technically superior that production might be on purely functional metrics.

These are not marginal or sentimental preferences. They are early signals of a fundamental reorientation of market value — one that will, over the coming years, accelerate as the supply of algorithmically generated cognitive output becomes effectively unlimited and the supply of genuinely human presence, genuinely human judgment, and genuinely human care remains, by definition, constrained. In a world where logic is a commodity and intuition is the new gold, the economics are not working against human beings. In the specific domains that matter most, they are working, for the first time in two centuries, in our favor.

IX. The Transition Problem: Living Between Worlds

Acknowledging the long-term reorientation of market value toward genuine human capabilities does not resolve the immediate and very real difficulty of the transition period — the years and decades during which the old economy's reward structures are dissolving faster than the new economies are solidifying. The person who has spent fifteen years building expertise in a field that AI is now disrupting cannot simply pivot to Human Premium activities based on an intellectual understanding that such activities will eventually be economically valued. They need to pay their rent now. They need to maintain their professional identity now. They need to find meaning and motivation now, in conditions that are neither the familiar stability of the pre-Efficiency Wall world nor the clarified landscape of the post-transition world.

The transition problem is real, and it would be dishonest to minimize it. Transitions of this magnitude — structural transformations in the organization of economic value that displace established professional identities in compressed timeframes — cause genuine suffering. Not the suffering of laziness or unwillingness to adapt, but the suffering of people who did everything they were told to do, built the skills and credentials and professional track records they were promised would protect them, and have discovered that the promise was underwritten by a set of economic assumptions that are no longer operative.

The honest response to this suffering is not to minimize it with reassurances about the long-term benefits of technological progress, nor to amplify it with catastrophizing about the permanent obsolescence of human value. It is to acknowledge it clearly, to understand its specific sources and mechanisms, and to offer what genuine support is available for navigating through it rather than merely around it.

Three things are genuinely helpful in the transition period. The first is an accurate understanding of what has changed and what has not — which is the purpose of this chapter. The Efficiency Wall is real. The threat to certain forms of market-valued cognitive expertise is real and not reversible. Clarity about this, however painful, is more useful than the false comfort of denial. What has not changed is the human capacity for the kinds of contribution that the Efficiency Wall cannot commoditize. These capacities are not new. They were not created by the crisis. They were always present, always genuinely valuable, always the most distinctively human things about human beings. The crisis has simply made their value legible in new ways.

The second thing that is genuinely helpful is community — specifically, the experience of navigating the transition in the company of others who are navigating it honestly, rather than in the isolation of private shame. The Identity Crash is, among other things, a profoundly lonely experience, because it attacks precisely the professional identity that is also the primary basis of most contemporary social connection. The colleagues, the professional networks, the LinkedIn connections — these are relationships organized around shared professional identity, and when that identity is threatened, the social structures that depended on it become correspondingly fragile. Building and maintaining relationships that are grounded in something more durable than professional identity — in genuine mutual knowledge, genuine shared values, and genuine care for each other's wellbeing beyond the dimensions of career success — is not merely a psychological luxury in the transition period. It is a survival resource.

The third thing that is genuinely helpful is the cultivation of the specific human capacities that the post-Efficiency Wall world will increasingly value — not as a calculated economic strategy, but as a genuine investment in the dimensions of oneself that the Church of the Grind systematically undervalued. The Deep Hour. The Physical Anchor. The Micro-Economy of Meaning. These practices, which are described in detail in Chapter Seven, are not merely therapies for the wounded professional identity. They are the building blocks of a different kind of identity altogether — one grounded in being rather than doing, in presence rather than performance, in the irreducibly human rather than the algorithmically approximable.

X. What Survives the Wall — and Why It Matters

Every genuine crisis contains within it, if examined honestly and without flinching, the seeds of something that the pre-crisis world was too comfortable to recognize, as necessary. The agricultural crisis of the fourteenth century — the catastrophic failure of crops across Europe that preceded and amplified the devastation of the Black Death — forced a fundamental restructuring of agricultural practice, breaking the grip of the three-field system that had been adequate for centuries but had become a source of fragility. The crisis of meaning that followed the Black Death itself forced a fundamental restructuring of the cosmological framework that had organized European civilization for a millennium, and in doing so created the conditions for the Renaissance.

The Efficiency Wall is a crisis of this order: not a temporary disruption that will resolve itself with a few years of adaptation, but a permanent transformation of the conditions under which human beings must find and create meaning. And like previous crises of this order, it contains within it the seeds of something that the pre-crisis world was too committed to its existing arrangements to recognize as possible.

What survives the Efficiency Wall — what is, in fact, revealed by the wall's existence to have always been present beneath the surface of the knowledge economy's cultural priorities — is the full dimensionality of human experience. Not the thin slice of human capability that the market for cognitive labor rewarded. Not the specific, narrowly defined professional competencies that the ten-thousand-hour rule promised to protect. But the whole, rich, irreducibly complex reality of what it is to be a human being: embodied, relational, creative, morally serious, capable of genuine love and genuine suffering and genuine wisdom earned through genuine engagement with the full spectrum of what a conscious life entails.

This is not a consolation prize for the economically displaced. It is the recognition of something that was always true and is now, for the first time in the history of industrial civilization, being forced into visibility by the very forces that seem most threatening to human significance. The machine that can think faster, more consistently, and with access to more information than any human being can match is also, in doing so, clarifying what thinking was never really the point of. What presence is. What connection is. What it means to be genuinely, irreducibly, and magnificently here.

The wall is not the end. It is the beginning of a clearer view.

CHAPTER THREE

THE GHOST IN THE OFFICE

✦✦✦

I. A HAUNTING WITHOUT A NAME

There is a particular species of professional suffering that has no entry in the Diagnostic and Statistical Manual of Mental Disorders, no recognized category in occupational health literature, and no culturally sanctioned vocabulary through which the person experiencing it can explain themselves to their physician, their manager, their spouse, or their own internal monologue. It is a suffering that announces itself not through the dramatic ruptures of breakdown or the visible symptoms of burnout, but through a slow, almost imperceptible erosion — a quiet leaching of substance from activities that once felt solid and significant, leaving behind a hollow structure that looks, from the outside, entirely intact.

The person who experiences this suffering goes to work. They attend their meetings. They complete their reports. They respond to their emails. They participate in their performance reviews, accept their promotions, and collect their salaries. By every external metric that the professional world uses to measure adequacy and achievement, they are functioning. They are, in the language of the organizational chart, successfully employed.

And yet, in the specific interior dimension that most determines whether a human life feels worth living, something has gone profoundly wrong. The activities that once generated genuine engagement — that once produced the experience of challenge met, of skill deployed, of contribution made — no longer do. The substance has been removed from the form. The meaning has evacuated the ritual. What remains is performance: the faithful reproduction of the external behaviors associated with professional engagement, in the absence of the internal experience that those behaviors were designed to express.

This is the condition that this chapter calls ghost employment. And the person living inside it is, in the most evocative and precise sense available, a ghost in the office. Not a lazy person, not a disengaged person, not a person who has simply stopped caring. A person whose core professional utility — the specific cognitive contribution that defined their role and anchored their identity — has been quietly, completely, and in many cases irreversibly absorbed by an automated system, while the organizational apparatus surrounding that contribution remains fully operational. The title remains. The salary continues. The role exists. The person is present. But the essential thing — the genuine human contribution that once gave all of it meaning — has already departed.

The ghost does not always know they have died. That is the most poignant feature of their situation. They continue going through the motions of professional life with the full sincerity of their pre-haunting selves, carrying the habits, the vocabulary, the professional reflexes of someone who is genuinely needed, genuinely contributing, genuinely essential to the enterprise that employs them. The discovery that none of this is quite true any longer — that the essential work is being done elsewhere, by a system that requires only occasional human supervision rather than sustained human intelligence — tends to arrive not as a single revelation but as a series of small, private, and deeply unsettling recognitions that accumulate over months or years before they coalesce into something that must be faced.

II. The Anatomy of Invisible Unemployment

The phrase "invisible unemployment" is chosen deliberately, and its precision is worth unpacking. It does not mean unemployment that is hidden in official statistics, though there is certainly an argument that official unemployment measures are failing to capture the full scope of the displacement underway. It means something more specific and more psychologically significant: the condition of being functionally unemployed — of having one's genuine productive contribution to one's organization reduced to near zero — while remaining nominally, contractually, and organizationally employed.

Conventional unemployment is, whatever its material hardships, at least legible. The person who has lost their job knows they have lost their job. They can grieve it, navigate the practical consequences, access the social support structures designed for their situation, and eventually begin the process of finding new employment or reorienting their professional life. The loss is real and often devastating, but it is named. It has a social category. It exists within a recognized framework of experience that, however inadequate, at least acknowledges the reality of what has happened.

Invisible unemployment offers none of these consolations. The person whose core professional function has been automated away while their organizational position remains intact cannot access the social vocabulary of job loss, because they have not lost their job. They cannot claim the legitimacy of unemployment because they are employed. They cannot grieve their professional displacement publicly, because publicly they appear entirely whole. What they can do — what many of them do, for years — is maintain the performance of professional engagement while the private experience of that engagement becomes progressively more hollow, more exhausting, and more corrosive to the sense of self that was built on the foundation of genuine contribution.

The mechanisms by which core professional function migrates from human to machine are varied, but the pattern they produce is remarkably consistent. In some cases the migration is sudden and visible: a specific AI system is deployed to perform a task that was previously performed by human beings, and the human beings are reassigned to supervisory or review roles. In others it is gradual and almost invisible: the tools available to professionals become progressively more capable, the fraction of work genuinely requiring human judgment progressively smaller, the time required for human review progressively shorter, until one day the professional realizes — if they allow themselves to realize it — that what once constituted a full day of meaningful cognitive work now constitutes, in substance, perhaps two hours of genuine engagement surrounded by six hours of elaborately organized waiting.

A senior financial analyst at a major investment bank described the experience to me with a precision that deserves to be quoted at length. "I used to spend two full days every week pulling apart the financials of a target company — really digging into the numbers, finding the things that weren't obvious, building a picture of what was going on beneath the reported figures. That was the job. That was the thing I was genuinely good at, that I'd spent years learning to do well. Now the system does all of that in about forty minutes, and my job is to check whether it missed anything. Which it almost never does. I sit there looking at this perfectly organized output, occasionally adding a note, and I think: for what am I here? And I don't have a satisfactory answer."

This experience — the experience of being present but not necessary, of occupying a role without inhabiting it — is the defining phenomenology of invisible unemployment. And the reason it is so psychologically damaging is precisely because it is invisible: because the person experiencing it has no legitimate grounds for complaint, no recognized framework for understanding their distress, and no sanctioned path toward resolution that does not require either a level of denial they can no longer sustain or a level of honesty that their organizational context cannot accommodate.

III. The Architecture of Bore-out

The clinical literature on workplace psychology has, for decades, focused its diagnostic and therapeutic attention overwhelmingly on burnout: the condition of chronic exhaustion, depersonalization, and reduced personal accomplishment that results from sustained exposure to important levels of workplace demand without adequate recovery resources. Burnout is real, thoroughly documented, widely recognized, and increasingly treated as a genuine occupational health concern rather than a personal weakness. It has a literature, a diagnostic framework, and a set of evidence-based interventions. It is, in the vocabulary of contemporary workplace wellbeing, a legitimate and socially recognized form of suffering.

Bore-out occupies a vastly different position in that vocabulary — or rather, it barely occupies a position at all. The term was coined by Swiss business consultants Philippe Rothlin and Peter Werder in their 2007 book of the same name, but it has never achieved the cultural traction of burnout, has never entered the mainstream vocabulary of occupational health, and remains, for most people who experience it, a condition without a name. This namelessness is not merely an inconvenience. It is a significant component of the condition's toxicity, because without a name, there is no legitimate framework for acknowledging the experience, no socially sanctioned permission to take it seriously, no recognized path toward addressing it.

Bore-out is defined as the psychological state resulting from chronic, sustained under-stimulation in the workplace: not the absence of tasks, but the absence of tasks that genuinely engage the person's cognitive, creative, or relational capacities. It is not laziness, and it is not the ordinary fatigue of a slow week or a routine assignment. It is the specific experience of being chronically required to perform activities that make no genuine demands on one's intelligence, judgment, creativity, or relational capacity — of operating, day after day, at a fraction of one's actual capability, without the prospect of genuine challenge or genuine contribution on the horizon.

The symptom profile of bore-out is, in some respects, paradoxically like that of burnout, which is one reason it is so frequently misdiagnosed. Both conditions produce fatigue, difficulty concentrating, emotional withdrawal, a sense of meaninglessness, and increasing reliance on distraction as a coping mechanism. The crucial distinction is in their etiology: burnout arises from too much of the wrong kind of demand, while bore-out arises from too little of the right kind. The treatment implications are diametrically opposed — which means that addressing bore-out with the interventions developed for burnout (rest, reduced workload, simplified demands) will not merely fail to help but will actively worsen the condition.

In the context of the Identity Crash, bore-out is becoming a mass professional experience rather than the occupational edge case it was when Rothlin and Werder first described it. As AI systems absorb the cognitively demanding components of knowledge work — the analysis, the synthesis, the pattern recognition, the drafting, the diagnosis, the strategic reasoning — what remains for the human beings in those roles is the cognitively undemanding: the review, the approval, the forwarding, the filing, the attending of meetings that exist primarily to maintain the social fiction of organizational activity. These are activities that require presence but not engagement, time but not attention, bodies in chairs but not minds genuinely at work.

The profound cruelty of bore-out, in this context, is that it precisely attacks the people who are most intellectually capable and most psychologically invested in their work. The person who is genuinely brilliant, genuinely curious, genuinely committed to contributing something of value — this person suffers bore-out most acutely, because the gap between what they are capable of and what is being asked of them is widest. The bore-out of the Identity Crash is, in this sense, an inversion of the familiar narrative of technological displacement: it is not primarily the least capable who are suffering most. It is the most capable, trapped in roles that no longer need their full capability, performing the rituals of engagement without the substance.

IV. Performative Labor and the Cost of Concealment

The term "performative labor" describes the activity — increasingly common in the era of invisible unemployment — of producing the appearance of productive work in the absence of its substance. It is the ghost's primary occupation: the sustained, effortful, psychologically expensive business of looking busy when the genuine busyness has departed.

Performative labor is not idleness. It is, in some respects, more exhausting than genuine work, because it layers atop the actual demands of the role an additional set of demands that are purely social and psychological: the demand to appear engaged, to signal investment, to generate the behavioral evidence of productivity in a context where the productivity itself is automated. The ghost who genuinely scrutinizes every AI-generated output — who reads every document, questions every recommendation, and brings their full critical intelligence to bear on everything that passes through their review queue — quickly falls behind a colleague who approves outputs in batches. The incentive structure rewards the performance of engagement over the substance of it.

The psychological cost of sustained performative labor is, in clinical terms, primarily a cost of cognitive dissonance: the chronic, unresolvable tension between one's self-concept as a genuine professional contributor and the lived reality of one's daily activities. Human beings are, neurologically and psychologically, extraordinarily sensitive to this kind of dissonance. The brain that understands itself to be capable of genuine contribution and finds itself instead performing an elaborate charade of contribution is not a brain that can simply decide to be comfortable with the discrepancy. It registers the dissonance as a low-grade but persistent alarm: something is wrong here, something is false here, something is being lost here that should not be lost.

Over time, this alarm produces a set of characteristic psychological responses that compound the original suffering. The first is shame: a private, often unacknowledged sense of fraudulence, of being an impostor in one's own professional life, of collecting a salary under false pretenses. This shame is particularly acute because its premises are, in a deep sense, correct — the person is, in fact, performing a role whose genuine content has been transferred to a machine — but its emotional valence is completely misdirected, because the fraudulence is structural rather than moral. The person did not choose to become a ghost. They were made into one by forces entirely beyond their control. But shame does not distinguish between structural conditions and personal failures. It attaches wherever there is a gap between appearance and reality, regardless of how that gap was created.

The second response is hypervigilance: a compensatory intensification of the performance of engagement, designed to preempt the discovery of the hollowness beneath it. The ghost who is most acutely aware of their own ghostliness is often, paradoxically, the most visibly "busy" person in the office: the one who sends emails at midnight, who volunteers for additional responsibilities, who maintains an elaborate display of professional activity that serves primarily as a screen against the recognition — by others and by themselves — that the essential thing is missing.

The third response, arriving later and often most destructively, is a kind of moral injury: a deep and persistent sense of having been wronged, not by any specific individual or identifiable malicious actor, but by the systems and structures and cultural expectations that promised that hard work, genuine commitment, and the development of genuine expertise would be adequately and durably rewarded. This is not entitlement. It is the specific suffering that arises when a contract that was believed to be real — that was built into one's life plan, one's identity, one's most fundamental assumptions about how the world works — turns out to have been underwritten by assumptions that are no longer operative. The suffering is real. The anger is legitimate. And it requires acknowledgment before it can be metabolized.

V. The Human-in-the-Loop: A Well-Intentioned Trap

The concept of "human-in-the-loop" AI — the principle that consequential automated decisions should be subject to human review, oversight, and approval before being acted upon — emerged from a genuine and important concern. As AI systems began to be deployed in contexts with significant real-world consequences — medical diagnosis, legal analysis, credit assessment, criminal justice risk scoring, autonomous vehicle operation — the question of how to maintain meaningful human accountability for algorithmically generated decisions became one of the central challenges of AI governance. The human-in-the-loop framework was developed as an answer to that challenge: keep a human being in the decision chain, ensure that the automation does not operate without human sanction, preserve the accountability that comes with human agency.

This is a genuinely important principle, and in domains where the consequences of automated error are severe and the capacity for meaningful human oversight is real, it is an essential safeguard. The surgeon who reviews an AI-generated diagnostic recommendation and brings their clinical judgment to bear on whether it fits the patient in front of them is performing genuine, irreplaceable, and consequential human review. The judge who examines an algorithmic sentencing recommendation and considers the full human context of the individual case is exercising a form of judgment that the algorithm cannot and should not replace.

But the human-in-the-loop framework, applied broadly and without discrimination across the full range of knowledge work, has also become, in practice, one of the primary mechanisms of ghost employment. And understanding why requires a clear-eyed examination of the conditions under which human-in-the-loop review constitutes genuine oversight rather than merely formal compliance with an organizational protocol.

Genuine human-in-the-loop review requires, at minimum, three things. It requires that the human reviewer have the expertise to meaningfully evaluate the automated output: to identify not merely obvious errors but the more subtle failures of context, judgment, and value that sophisticated AI systems are most prone to. It requires that the reviewer have the time to exercise that expertise: to read, consider, question, and when necessary override the automated recommendation, rather than approving it as a matter of throughput management. And it requires that the organizational incentive structure genuinely rewards substantive review rather than merely nominal approval: that the reviewer who consistently challenges and sometimes overrides the AI system is valued as a critical quality control resource rather than penalized as a bottleneck in the production process.

In practice, these three conditions are rarely all present simultaneously. The volume of AI-generated output in most modern knowledge work organizations has grown faster than the human capacity to review it with genuine depth. The expertise required to meaningfully evaluate sophisticated AI outputs in many domains is itself increasingly rare, as the training pipelines for that expertise have been disrupted by the very automation whose outputs need to be reviewed. And the organizational incentive structures of most institutions reward speed and throughput over depth and criticality, creating systematic pressure toward the nominal approval of AI-generated outputs rather than their genuine scrutiny.

The result is a widespread institutional fiction: organizations that believe they have maintained meaningful human oversight of their automated systems, staffed by individuals who believe they are performing meaningful professional roles, when what is occurring is a sophisticated performance of oversight that has little substantive connection to the quality of the automated decisions being "reviewed." The human is in the loop, but the loop has been drawn so large and traversed so quickly that the human's presence in it has become, for practical purposes, ceremonial.

This is not a description of individual failure. It is a description of a systemic condition that emerges inevitably from the interaction of rapidly improving AI capability, organizational pressures toward efficiency, and the institutional inertia that keeps role structures in place long after the substance those structures were designed to house has migrated elsewhere. The individuals caught in this condition are not lazy, not incompetent, and not responsible for the structural circumstances that produced it. They are, in the most precise sense, victims of an organizational transition that has not yet developed the vocabulary, the frameworks, or the institutional will to honestly acknowledge what it is doing to the human beings it nominally employs.

VI. The Specific Grief of the Displaced Expert

Among all the psychological dimensions of ghost employment, the most consistently underestimated and underacknowledged is the genuine grief that accompanies the displacement of expertise. Not the grief of economic loss, though that is real and significant. Not the grief of status reduction, though that is also real. But the specific, intimate grief of having spent years developing a genuine capability — of having learned to do something difficult and important with real mastery — and then watching that capability become, not merely less economically valuable, but redundant in the daily activity of one's professional life.

Expertise is not merely a professional asset. For the person who has genuinely developed it, expertise is a form of identity, a mode of being in the world, a specific way of seeing and engaging with a domain of reality that has been built through years of sustained, often painful attention. The expert radiologist who has spent fifteen years learning to read medical images does not merely possess a skill in the way one might possess a certification or a tool. They have developed a perceptual capacity — a trained ability to notice patterns in visual data that are invisible to the untrained eye — that has become part of how they experience the world. Their expertise is not something they do. It is, in a meaningful sense, something they are.

When an AI vision system achieves diagnostic accuracy on standard imaging tasks that matches or exceeds that of experienced radiologists — as multiple studies have now demonstrated in specific domains — the economic implications are significant. But the psychological implications for the radiologist who has organized their identity around the exercise of that perceptual expertise, are of a different order entirely. What is being displaced is not merely a job function. It is a way of being valuable in the world — a specific form of contribution that was understood to be both genuinely important and genuinely the product of one's own developed capacity. Its displacement by a machine does not merely reduce one's economic security. It raises, with brutal directness, the question of whether those years of development — those tens of thousands of hours of training, the sacrifices made, the identity built — were, in some essential sense, spent on something that turned out not to need them.

This is the grief that has no social recognition and no legitimate vocabulary. It is the grief of the craftsperson whose craft has been industrialized, the musician whose instrument has been synthesized, the navigator whose charts have been replaced by GPS. It is a grief that is complicated by the fact that the displacement is, in many respects, genuinely good: better medical diagnoses, faster legal processing, more accessible financial analysis, more efficient code generation. The outcomes the automation produces are, by measurable standards, often superior to the outcomes the human experts produced. The ghost has no standing to claim that the machine is worse. They can only claim, in the privacy of their own experience, that something has been lost that cannot be measured — and that what has been lost was, for them, the point.

Acknowledging this grief is not self-indulgence. It is a necessary precondition for genuine adaptation. The person who bypasses the grief — who accepts the organizational narrative that they are still valuable, still necessary, still performing a meaningful role, without honestly examining whether that narrative corresponds to their actual experience — will not adapt. They will perform adaptation while remaining, in a deeper sense, stuck. The grief must be felt, named, and metabolized before the genuine work of reimagining professional identity can begin. This is not a comfortable process, and there is no shortcut through it. But there is a passage, and on the other side of it lies something more genuinely valuable than the expertise that was lost.

VII. Organizational Denial and Its Costs

The ghost in the office does not haunt themselves only. They inhabit an organizational ecosystem that is, in most cases, engaged in its own form of denial: a collective, institutionally sanctioned fiction about the continued relevance and genuine contribution of roles that have been substantively hollowed out by automation. Understanding this organizational dimension of invisible unemployment is essential, both for diagnosing the full scope of the problem and for understanding why it is so resistant to individual solutions.

Organizations have powerful incentives to maintain the fiction of continued human relevance in automated workflows. Some of these incentives are regulatory: in many industries and jurisdictions, the deployment of automated decision-making in consequential domains requires evidence of meaningful human oversight, and the formal maintenance of human-in-the-loop roles serves as that evidence, regardless of whether the oversight is substantive. Some are reputational: the public acknowledgment that a sizable portion of one's workforce is performing roles whose genuine content has been automated away would generate negative press, employee relations crises, and potential legal exposure that organizations prefer to avoid.

Some, more subtly, are psychological: organizations are themselves collections of human beings with identities, self-concepts, and needs for coherence, and the honest acknowledgment that a major organizational function has been automated in ways that render the human beings who previously performed it genuinely redundant is, for organizational leaders who also have human identities and human needs for self-coherence, a deeply uncomfortable reckoning. It is easier, and in the short term less costly, to maintain the fiction that everyone is still doing important work, to redescribe automated functions as "AI-assisted" professional roles, and to invest in the performance of organizational health rather than in its substance.

The costs of this organizational denial are both direct and indirect. The direct costs are the ongoing salary and benefits expenses of maintaining positions whose genuine productive content has been automated away — a real but, in the short term, manageable expense that organizations can absorb as a cost of organizational stability and regulatory compliance. The indirect costs are more significant and more damaging: the psychological deterioration of the workforce caught in the fiction, the erosion of genuine organizational intelligence as the human beings who might otherwise be contributing genuine judgment and creativity are instead occupied with the performance of redundant oversight, and the progressive atrophy of the institutional capacity for honest self-assessment that would be necessary to navigate the transition successfully.

Most significantly, organizational denial prevents the development of the new organizational forms — the new roles, the new frameworks for contribution, the new ways of structuring and valuing human work in an AI-augmented environment — that are urgently needed. The organization that maintains the fiction of continued business-as-usual, redescribing automated functions as human roles without genuinely rethinking what human contribution in an AI-augmented context consists of, is not adapting. It is deferring the reckoning, accumulating the costs of the deferral, and ensuring that when the reckoning finally arrives, it will be more severe than it needed to be.

VIII. The Social Dimensions of Haunting

Ghost employment is not only a private psychological experience. It has significant social dimensions that shape how the condition is experienced, how it is communicated (or not communicated), and what resources are available for navigating it. These social dimensions deserve explicit examination, because they are among the most important determinants of whether the ghost's experience remains a private, isolating suffering or becomes the beginning of a more genuinely collective reckoning with the conditions producing it.

The primary social dimension of ghost employment is isolation. The condition produces isolation for structural reasons: the very nature of invisible unemployment makes it impossible to discuss with others, because the standard vocabulary of professional difficulty does not fit and the standard social supports for professional distress are not available. You cannot tell your colleagues that you feel like a ghost in your own office without risking either the exposure of a vulnerability that could be professionally damaging or the triggering of a defensive organizational response that will make your situation worse rather than better. You cannot tell your manager that your role has been substantively automated away without initiating a conversation whose outcomes you cannot predict and may not be able to control. You cannot tell your partner or your friends without generating either well-meaning but inadequate reassurance or genuine anxiety about the economic implications.

The result is a pervasive silence around one of the most widespread forms of professional suffering of the current era. People who are experiencing ghost employment are, in most cases, experiencing it alone — not because they are alone in their experience, but because the social conditions for acknowledging and sharing that experience do not exist in most of the contexts they inhabit. The isolation compounds the suffering in ways that are well-documented in the psychology of concealed distress: the energy required to maintain the concealment depletes the resources available for coping with the underlying condition, while the absence of social support and genuine acknowledgment prevents the validation and normalization that would make the experience less damaging.

What breaks the isolation, when it is broken, is almost always the discovery of others in the same condition — usually occurring informally, in the specific social settings where professional defenses are lowered enough to permit genuine honesty: the late-evening conversation at a conference, the candid exchange with a former colleague who has already left the organization, the support group that has no formal name but is effectively constituted by the small group of colleagues who have begun, in private, to acknowledge what they are actually experiencing. These informal communities of shared recognition are, for many people navigating ghost employment, the first and most valuable resource available. They provide what the formal organizational and clinical support structures cannot: the experience of being genuinely seen and genuinely understood by someone else who knows, from the inside, what it is like.

The social dimension of ghost employment also has a generational dimension that is worth acknowledging. The experience of discovering that the professional identity one has spent years building has been made partially or substantially redundant is differently inflected depending on where one is in the arc of a professional life. For the early-career professional who has not yet fully invested in a specific professional identity, the discovery may arrive as a useful early warning: a prompt to orient toward the dimensions of human contribution that the Efficiency Wall cannot commoditize before the investment in the wrong identity has been made. For the mid-career professional who has spent a decade or more building specific expertise and organizational capital, the experience is more genuinely disorienting: the investment is substantial, the identity is established, and the prospect of a fundamental reorientation is both challenging and personally threatening. For the late-career professional who has spent three or four decades building a professional identity and is now watching it dissolve in the final years before retirement, the experience can have a quality of tragedy that the younger person's situation does not carry.

Each of these generational experiences requires different forms of acknowledgment and different forms of support. The early-career person needs guidance toward the genuine human capabilities that are worth investing in. The mid-career person needs both honest acknowledgment of what has been lost and genuine support for the complicated process of reorientation. The late-career person needs the validation of a life's work that remains genuinely valuable regardless of whether its specific market form has been disrupted. What all of them share is the need for a social context in which their experience is recognized as real, legitimate, and worthy of genuine engagement — rather than minimized, dismissed, or redirected toward productivity optimization strategies that miss the point entirely.

IX. From Process Manager to Meaning Maker: The Transformation

The path out of ghost employment is not a career pivot, a retraining program, or an organizational restructuring, though any of these may be components of the journey for specific individuals. It is a more fundamental transformation: a shift in the organizing principle of one's professional identity from what might be called Process Management to what this book calls Meaning Making.

Process Management is the mode of professional contribution that the knowledge economy built its reward structures around: the reliable, expert, efficient execution of defined cognitive tasks within established frameworks. The financial analyst who produces accurate market analyses. The lawyer who drafts compliant legal documents. The diagnostician who reads imaging studies correctly. The software engineer who writes functional code. These are process management contributions: valuable, trained, and essential to organizational functioning — and, in their specific cognitive content, increasingly approximable by AI systems that can execute the same processes faster, more consistently, and at lower marginal cost.

Meaning Making is the mode of professional contribution that the post-Efficiency Wall world increasingly requires and rewards, but that the organizational structures and cultural frameworks of the knowledge economy have never adequately recognized, measured, or compensated. The Meaning Maker is not primarily an executor of defined processes. They are a navigator of human context: the person in the organization who understands not merely what the data says but what it means for the specific human beings whose lives will be affected by the decisions it informs. The person who can hold the complexity of competing values, the weight of genuine consequences, and the irreducible particularity of specific human situations in a way that no optimization algorithm can approximate.

The Meaning Maker asks the questions that the AI system cannot ask, because they are not questions about data. They are questions about people. Not "what is the optimal solution?" but "optimal for whom, and at whose expense?" Not "what does the analysis indicate?" but "what is the analysis failing to capture about the human reality it purports to describe?" Not "what is the most efficient process?" but "what does this process do to the human beings who participate in it, and is that acceptable?" These are questions that require not merely intelligence but wisdom: the specific form of understanding that emerges from having lived a human life, with its full complement of experience, error, loss, and growth.

The transition from Process Manager to Meaning Maker is not a simple reorientation. It requires, first, the honest acknowledgment that the Process Management identity has been displaced — which means going through the grief described in earlier sections rather than defending against it. It requires, second, a genuine investment in the development of the capabilities that Meaning Making requires: the deepened capacity for human attention, for ethical reasoning, for the kind of contextual judgment that comes from genuine engagement with the full complexity of human situations rather than the simplified versions that data models can capture. And it requires, third, the courage to occupy a professional role whose contributions are less easily measured, less neatly defined, and less immediately legible in organizational terms than the process management role it replaces.

This courage is not a minor requirement. In organizational cultures built around the measurement and management of defined outputs, the Meaning Maker's contribution is systematically hard to recognize and systematically easy to dismiss. The person who raises the human implications of an algorithmically generated recommendation, who insists on the importance of contextual factors that the model did not capture, who slows the decision process down in the name of genuine consideration of the people it will affect — this person is, in the logic of the productivity-focused organization, a friction point. A source of inefficiency. A bottleneck in the process.

That this person is also, in the logic of genuine organizational health and genuine human flourishing, the most valuable person in the room — is a truth that many organizations will be slow to recognize and slower still to act on. But it is a truth that the individuals navigating the Identity Crash do not need to wait for organizational recognition to act on. The transition from Process Manager to Meaning Maker begins not with a job change or an organizational restructuring, but with a personal decision: to be genuinely present, genuinely attentive, and genuinely committed to the human dimensions of one's work, regardless of whether the organizational culture has yet developed the capacity to reward that commitment.

X. Leaving the Haunted House

The metaphor of the ghost in the office, like all useful metaphors, eventually reaches the limit of its applicability. Ghosts, in the traditional understanding of the figure, are defined by their inability to leave: they are bound to the site of their haunting by some unresolved attachment, some unacknowledged reality, some incomplete reckoning that keeps them circling the same rooms, performing the same actions, unable to move on. The ghost in the office is different from this in one crucial respect: they can leave. The haunting is not permanent. The house can be exited.

But exiting it requires something that the traditional ghost story does not prepare us for: it requires the ghost to first fully acknowledge that they are haunting. To name, honestly and without flinching, the reality that the role they are performing is more form than substance, that the professional identity they are maintaining is organized around a contribution that has been automated away, and that continuing to circle the same rooms is not sustaining them but depleting them.

This acknowledgment is, in practice, the hardest part of the transition. It requires a level of honest self-assessment that runs directly against the grain of organizational culture, professional socialization, and the deep psychological need to maintain the self-concept of a capable and genuinely contributing professional. It requires the willingness to feel, fully and without premature resolution, the grief, the shame, the anger, and the disorientation of the Identity Crash in its specific professional manifestation. And it requires, most demandingly, the willingness to sit with the uncertainty of not yet knowing what comes next — to occupy the space between the old identity and the new one without filling it prematurely with either denial or despair.

What the chapters that follow offer is a map for navigating that uncertain space. Not a prescription that guarantees safe arrival at a predetermined destination, but an honest account of the terrain, the hazards, and the resources that are genuinely available to the person who is willing to make the journey. The Worth Paradox. The Dopamine Trap. The Human Renaissance. The Post-Utility Blueprint. Each of these is a chapter in the story of what becomes possible once the haunting has been honestly named and the house has been genuinely exited.

The ghost who walks out of the office does not walk into nothing. They walk into the full dimensionality of a human life that was always larger than the role that had been carved out for them within the organizational structure of a knowledge economy that valued them for what they could process rather than for what they could be. What they can be — what any human being can be, freed from the narrowing demands of the Church of the Grind and the specific professional identity it sanctioned — is something far more interesting, far more durable, and far more genuinely valuable than the process manager they were trained to become.

The haunted house is not the only house available. And the first step toward the door is always the same: the willingness to see clearly where you are.

The lights in the towers are still on. But the ghosts are learning to leave

CHAPTER FOUR

THE WORTH PARADOX

✦ ✦ ✦

There is a peculiar feature of the current technological moment that distinguishes it from every previous wave of automation in human history, and that peculiarity is the source of what we might call the Worth Paradox.

Previous waves of automation — the mechanization of agriculture in the nineteenth century, the automation of factory labor in the twentieth — were visible. Their effects were concentrated in specific industries, specific communities, and specific classes of workers. The people displaced could, however painfully, point to the machines that had displaced them. They could organize, protest, relocate, and retrain. The disruption was real and often brutal, but it was legible.

The current wave of automation is different in kind, not merely in degree. It is displacing not the labor of hands and bodies — though it is doing that too — but the labor of minds. And the displacement of mental labor is, by its nature, far harder to see, far harder to name, and far harder to grieve publicly. When a factory closes, the community mourns together. When a cognitive skill becomes economically obsolete, the displacement is experienced in private, in silence, and with a peculiar overlay of shame — because it feels less like being replaced by a machine than like being outperformed by one.

The Worth Paradox is this: the more efficiently AI produces the outputs that our economy has traditionally valued, the less necessary individual human beings feel in the production of those outputs. This is paradoxical because the outputs themselves are not less valuable. If anything, they are more abundant, more accessible, and more widely distributed than at any previous moment in history. The world is richer. And yet the people in it feel poorer, in the specific currency of felt purpose and personal significance. We have created an engine of abundance, and it has given us Uselessness Syndrome.

I. The Historical Roots of Worth

To understand why the Worth Paradox cuts so deeply, we need to understand how deeply the equation of worth with economic utility is embedded in Western culture — not as a natural truth, but as a historical construction that took centuries to build and has become so familiar we mistake it for nature itself.

The philosopher Max Weber famously traced the origins of modern capitalism's moral energy to what he called the Protestant ethic. For the reformers of the sixteenth and seventeenth centuries, especially the Calvinist strand, the question of salvation was agonizing and unanswerable: you could not know whether you were among the elect. But there was one signal, one earthly indicator that offered a degree of comfort: worldly success in your calling. Diligent, productive labor was not a means of earning salvation — Calvin was emphatic about this — but it was evidence of a character that God had blessed.

Over the following two centuries, this theological framework underwent a remarkable secularization. The salvation anxiety faded, but the moral significance of productive labor remained. Demanding work retained its halo even after the theology that had created the halo was forgotten. By the time industrial capitalism arrived in earnest in the nineteenth century, the equation was complete: a person's worth — their moral value, their social standing, their right to dignity and respect — was measured by their productive contribution. Not by what they were. By what they produced.

This equation served industrial capitalism extraordinarily well. A society of people who believed that their worth was contingent on their output was a society that would work tirelessly, tolerate harsh conditions, and feel personally ashamed — rather than politically indignant — when the economic system failed to reward their labor. The ideology of meritocracy, which became the dominant secular religion of the twentieth century, was the final refinement: it added the claim that the equation was not merely descriptive but just. You were worth what you earned because you earned what you were worth.

> *We mistake a historical construction for a natural truth. The equation of worth with output was built by specific people in specific circumstances, for specific purposes. It can be unmade.*

It is worth pausing here to feel the full weight of what this history implies. The sense of worthlessness that millions of people are experiencing in the face of AI-driven automation is not a natural response to a natural situation. It is the specific product of a specific ideological inheritance — one that was never universally shared across cultures or time periods, and that is, in any case, philosophically indefensible. The person who feels diminished because an AI can write the report faster than they can is not perceiving a truth about their worth. They are experiencing the collision between a technological reality and a historical ideology. And only one of those things is inevitable.

THE DIGNITY OF CRAFT BEFORE INDUSTRIALISM

It is instructive to consider what 'worth' meant before industrial capitalism colonized the concept. In the medieval guild system, worth was bound not to output — not to the quantity of goods produced — but to mastery: the deep knowledge of a craft, the embodied skill that took years to acquire, the relationship between a master craftsman and the material they shaped. A master shoemaker was not valued for the number of shoes they could produce per day. They were valued for their understanding of leather, their knowledge of the human foot, their capacity to solve problems that no amount of speed or volume could substitute for.

This conception of worth was not egalitarian — the guild system was hierarchical and often exclusionary — but it was, in one crucial respect, more philosophically coherent than the industrial conception that replaced it. It located worth in what a person knew and could do, in the depth of their engagement with their craft, rather than in the quantity of their output. It was resistant, in a way that the industrial conception was not, to displacement by automation. You could not replace a master craftsman with a faster version of the same thing, because what the craftsman offered was not merely speed or volume but depth and judgment.

The industrial revolution did not simply automate tasks. It restructured the entire conception of what human labor was for — and what human workers were worth. It was, in this sense, the first Worth Paradox: an explosion of productive capacity that left the people who had built their identities around a different kind of productive engagement feeling displaced, degraded, and confused. The Luddites were not opposed to technology in the abstract. They were grieving the destruction of a way of working — and a way of being — that had defined their dignity.

II. The Cognitive Architecture of Self-Worth

Understanding the Worth Paradox requires moving from history to psychology — specifically, to what researchers have learned in recent decades about how human beings construct and maintain their sense of self-worth.

The foundational distinction in this literature is between what psychologists call contingent self-worth and what we might, for contrast, call grounded self-worth. Contingent self-worth is the pattern in which a person's sense of their own value fluctuates in direct response to their performance in specific domains: career achievement, physical appearance, social approval, academic performance, and so on. Grounded self-worth, by contrast, is stable and independent of performance outcomes. A person with grounded self-worth can fail at a task, face rejection, or experience setbacks without experiencing these events as existential threats.

Research consistently shows that contingent self-worth, while often motivating in the short term, is psychologically costly. People with important levels of contingent self-worth experience greater anxiety, greater emotional volatility, greater vulnerability to depression, and —

paradoxically — worse performance in the domains they care most about. When your self-esteem is riding on your next performance review, the performance review becomes a source of existential threat rather than useful feedback, and existential threat does not bring out the best in human cognition.

THE NEUROSCIENCE OF CONTINGENT WORTH

Recent neuroscientific research has begun to illuminate the neural underpinnings of these psychological patterns. When a person with high contingent self-worth in the professional domain encounters evidence that their professional contribution is less valuable than they believed — a negative evaluation, a competitor outperforming them, or, increasingly, a demonstration that an AI can replicate their work — the brain's threat-detection systems activate in a way that is structurally similar to physical threat.

The amygdala, which processes emotional significance and threat, shows heightened activation. The prefrontal cortex, which handles complex reasoning and perspective-taking, shows reduced activity. The person becomes, in neurological terms, less capable of the nuanced thinking that might help them navigate the situation wisely — at precisely the moment when nuanced thinking is most needed.

This is not a flaw in human cognition. It is, in evolutionary terms, a feature: the brain prioritizes survival over complexity when it detects threats. But the threat-detection system evolved for physical threats, not for threats to the abstract sense of economic value. The result is that the experience of professional displacement activates the same survival circuitry as a physical attack — producing the same desperate quality of response, the same tunnel vision, the same urgency that crowds out everything else.

The brain cannot easily distinguish between 'my career is threatened' and 'my life is threatened.' This is why the Worth Paradox feels so visceral — because, neurologically, it is.

Understanding this architecture is not merely intellectually interesting. It has direct practical implications. If the sense of worthlessness produced by AI-driven displacement is, at least in part, a neurological threat response, then managing it requires — among other things — techniques that down-regulate that threat response: restoring prefrontal cortex activity, reducing amygdala reactivity, and creating the psychological spaciousness in which more nuanced and constructive responses become possible. We will return to these techniques in a later section.

The Construction of the Professional Self

In most contemporary Western societies, the professional self — the identity built around one's role, function, and contribution in the economic domain — occupies a position of unusual psychological centrality. Research by sociologist Arlie Hochschild and others has documented the degree to which middle-class professional culture in the late twentieth century encouraged people to invest their deepest selfhood in their work. The office became not merely a place of employment but a community, a source of meaning, a stage for the performance of the most important aspects of one's identity.

This investment was not irrational. For many people, their work genuinely offered the most consistent source of mastery, social connection, structured purpose, and recognized contribution available to them. A society that had dismantled other frameworks for identity — extended family networks, religious community, durable geographic roots — had, by default, elevated the workplace to fill the vacuum.

The cognitive consequence of this elevation is a professional identity that is not merely important to the person but constitutive of them — the foundation on which the entire edifice of self is built. When that foundation is threatened, the threat is not to a part of the self. It is to the whole.

III. THE SHAME ECONOMY: WHY COGNITIVE DISPLACEMENT IS UNIQUELY SILENCING

There is a dimension of the current disruption that distinguishes it from previous episodes of technological unemployment and that has received insufficient attention: the extraordinary capacity of cognitive displacement to produce shame.

When a factory worker is displaced by a machine, the displacement is public. The factory closes. The community suffers together. The displaced worker is, in a genuine sense, part of a visible collective — a group of people who can march, organize, demand, and grieve together. The cause of their displacement is concrete: a machine, a corporate decision, a trade policy. The displacement is not personal. It happened to everyone.

When a knowledge worker's skills are displaced by AI, none of this is available. The displacement is often invisible — a slow erosion of significance rather than a sudden loss of income. The person continues to work. They are still employed. They may be, by conventional metrics, quite successful. And yet they feel a growing, corrosive suspicion that what they are doing no longer matters in the way it once did — that the value they believed they were adding has been quietly absorbed by systems that do not need them.

This suspicion is profoundly difficult to articulate publicly, for a simple reason: in the dominant cultural framework, the appropriate response to the threat of obsolescence is to adapt, upskill, and outperform. The culture of meritocracy insists that the problem is always, at least in part, a personal failure — a failure to learn fast enough, change adeptly enough, position oneself cleverly enough. To admit that you feel threatened by AI is, in this framework, to admit inadequacy. And so the displacement goes underground, expressed not as political grievance or collective protest but as private anxiety, imposter syndrome, and the specific, corrosive despair of the person who is trying hard and increasingly unsure why.

THE SILENCE OF THE SUCCESSFUL

The most striking feature of the shame economy is that it is most powerful among those who are, by conventional measures, most successful. A mid-level analyst who has watched AI take over their spreadsheet work can point to the change and articulate their anxiety. A senior partner at a law firm, a chief strategy officer, a tenured professor — these people face a more complex and in some ways more destabilizing version of the same threat, because the gap between their self-image and their perceived dispensability is so much wider.

The psychologist Jennifer Crocker, one of the leading researchers on contingent self-worth, has documented what she calls the 'high-stakes trap': the pattern in which the higher the stakes attached to a performance domain, the more psychologically devastating threats to that domain become. The knowledge worker who has built an entire identity around their cognitive contribution — who has told themselves for decades that their intelligence and judgment set them apart — faces, in the emergence of genuinely capable AI, not merely a career challenge but a narrative crisis. The story they have been telling about themselves, which is also the story that has organized their sense of purpose, their social relationships, and their sense of their own future, is suddenly in question in a way it has never been before.

This is the shame economy: a cultural system in which the most legitimate response to structural displacement — collective acknowledgment, political organizing, shared grief — is foreclosed by an ideology of individual responsibility, leaving each displaced person to experience their displacement as personal failure, in private, and without the resources that solidarity might provide.

IV. The Anatomy of Uselessness Syndrome

Uselessness Syndrome is not a clinical diagnosis. It is a descriptive term for a constellation of psychological experiences that emerge when the traditional sources of self-worth — productive contribution to a valued activity — are eroded or eliminated by external forces beyond one's control.

Its symptoms are recognizable to anyone who has lived through a period of sustained unemployment or disability — but with a crucial additional dimension. The person experiencing Uselessness Syndrome is not, in most cases, unemployed. They are working. They are, often, quite productive by conventional measures. The syndrome arises not from the absence of activity but from the growing suspicion that the activity no longer matters — that it could be done better, faster, and without them.

Five Faces of Uselessness Syndrome

Uselessness Syndrome manifests differently depending on personality, professional context, and the domain in which the displacement is felt. The following five portraits are composites drawn from patterns observed across numerous conversations and contexts, offered not as clinical case studies but as portraits of recognition — ways of seeing yourself, or someone you know, in the texture of an experience that is rarely described accurately.

The first face is The Accelerator. This is the person who responds to the threat of AI displacement by working harder, faster, and more obsessively than ever before. They are easy to miss as someone in distress because their distress is entirely invisible beneath the hyperactivity it produces. They are first in the office and last to leave. They respond to emails at midnight. They take on more projects than any human being can complete, because activity — pure, exhausting, relentless activity — is the only thing that quiets the whisper that none of it matters. The Accelerator is not lazy. They are terrified. And their terror has taken the form of a productivity that is, paradoxically, the most efficient path to burnout.

The second face is The Perfectionist. This person's response to the AI threat is precision: if they cannot compete on volume or speed, they will compete on quality. They revise everything multiple times. They are never satisfied with good enough. Every output is a defense against the suspicion that without their exacting standards — standards that, they tell themselves, no AI could match — they would have nothing to offer. The Perfectionist's suffering is intimate and exhausting, lived in the gap between the standard they are trying to reach and the work they can produce. They are often high performers by conventional measures. They are never happy.

The third face is The Avoider. Where the Accelerator responds to threat by doing more, the Avoider responds by doing less. They procrastinate, defer decisions, and find elaborate reasons why the project is not yet ready to begin. Their avoidance is not laziness — it is, at a deeper level, a refusal to produce evidence that can be judged. If they never finish the report, it can never be found wanting. If they never complete the project, no AI can be set alongside it as a comparison. The Avoider is protecting the last thing they feel they can protect: the possibility, still intact as long as the work remains undone, that they might be excellent.

The fourth face is The Nostalgist. This person has not lost the capacity to work effectively; they have lost the desire. They remember a time when the work felt different — when the effort required felt proportionate to the significance of the output, when the gap between the work and the tool was not so humiliatingly vast. They speak often of how things used to be, how craftsmanship used to matter, how the profession used to require something that it no longer seems to require. Their grief is real and legitimate. But it has calcified into a posture, and the posture is beginning to cost them relationships and opportunities they cannot afford to lose.

The fifth face is The Philosopher. This person has arrived, often painfully, at a kind of intellectual detachment from the whole domain of professional identity. They speak about the disruption with apparent equanimity — sometimes with a wry, almost amused resignation. They quote thinkers about the absurdity of attachment to outcomes. They seem, in conversations about the future of work, to be the calmest person in the room. What they often cannot admit — sometimes even to themselves — is that the detachment is not genuine philosophical serenity but a defense mechanism: a way of ensuring that what they care about can no longer hurt them, by the simple expedient of pretending they no longer care.

V. The Radical Act: Decoupling Worth from Utility

The solution to the Worth Paradox — the only genuine solution, as opposed to the temporary relief of distraction or the false comfort of denial — is what might be called the most radical act available to a twenty-first century human being:

Decouple your sense of worth from your utility to the market.

This is radical because everything about the culture we have inherited — the Church of the Grind in all its manifestations — actively, insistently, and sometimes viciously resists this decoupling. To decouple worth from utility is not to abandon productivity or to celebrate idleness. It is to perform a precise cognitive reorganization — to move the foundation of one's self-evaluation from the domain of output to the domain of being.

This reorganization requires what psychologists call a 're-appraisal' of the meaning of worth itself. Not a superficial reassurance that 'you are enough just as you are' — which, however well-intentioned, tends to ring hollow against the backdrop of genuine economic precarity — but a genuine, worked-through understanding of why the concept of human worth was always poorly served by the productivity metric, even when that metric was economically dominant.

What the Decoupling Is Not

Before describing what the decoupling involves, it is important to be clear about what it is not — because the idea is frequently misunderstood in ways that make it seem either impossibly demanding or, conversely, suspiciously easy.

The decoupling is not a claim that your work does not matter. It matters enormously. The way you spend your working hours shapes your life, your relationships, your sense of engagement with the world, and your contribution to the people around you. None of that significance is diminished by decoupling your fundamental worth from the market value of your outputs. What changes is the direction of causation: rather than deriving your worth from your work, you bring your worth to your work. The difference is not semantic. It is the difference between a foundation and a weather vane.

The decoupling is not a counsel of passivity. It does not suggest that you should stop developing skills, stop caring about performance, or stop seeking to contribute effectively. On the contrary: people who have genuinely decoupled their worth from their utility are, eventually, more effective contributors than those who have not. When your self-esteem is not riding on every output, you can take the risks, accept the failures, and engage with the feedback that genuine growth requires.

The decoupling is not a luxury available only to the financially secure. This is the most important misunderstanding to address because it is the one most likely to make the idea feel irrelevant to people experiencing genuine economic precarity. Your economic situation is real, and the anxiety it produces is legitimate. The decoupling does not deny this. What it challenges is the conflation of economic precarity with personal worthlessness — the assumption that because your economic situation is uncertain, you are uncertain as a person. These are different problems, and they require different responses.

You can be economically vulnerable and still be, without qualification or asterisk, a person of full and unconditional worth. The market does not issue certificates of personhood.

VI. What Philosophers Knew

The insight that human worth cannot be adequately grounded in utility or productivity is not new. It is, in fact, one of the oldest and most consistently argued positions in the entire history of human thought. What is new is only the urgency with which the material conditions of the early twenty-first century are forcing the question back onto the agenda.

Aristotle and the Life of Flourishing

Aristotle's concept of eudaimonia — often translated as 'happiness' but more accurately rendered as 'flourishing' or 'living well' — was explicitly constructed as an alternative to accounts of the good life that reduced it to pleasure, wealth, or external success. For Aristotle, eudaimonia was an activity: the ongoing exercise of distinctively human capacities — reason, social engagement, moral virtue, contemplation — in a way that expressed their fullest development. It was not the state you reached; it was the way you lived.

What is particularly relevant to the Worth Paradox is Aristotle's insistence that eudaimonia could not be taken from you by external circumstances. A man who had lost his fortune, his social position, even his health could still, in Aristotle's account, live well — if he continued to exercise the virtues that constituted the deepest expression of his humanity. This was not merely consolation philosophy. It was a carefully worked-out argument that the things most people ran after — wealth, status, the esteem of others — were not the things that constituted genuine flourishing, but merely the material conditions that could make it easier or harder to pursue.

Aristotle would have had a precise diagnosis for the Worth Paradox: it is the confusion of external goods — the outputs and achievements by which the market assigns value — with the internal goods that constitute a genuinely worthwhile life. The confusion is ancient. What is new is the form it takes when the market's capacity to value your outputs is suddenly and dramatically disrupted.

VIKTOR FRANKL AND THE IRREDUCIBILITY OF MEANING

Viktor Frankl's experience as a psychiatrist in the Nazi concentration camps led him to a conclusion that is directly relevant to the Worth Paradox: that human beings can endure almost any material deprivation if they retain a sense of meaning, and that meaning is not derived from external circumstances but chosen by the individual in response to those circumstances.

Frankl's key insight — the insight that his logotherapy was built on — was that between stimulus and response there is a space, and in that space lies the human being's freedom to choose their orientation toward their experience. This is not the freedom to change the circumstances — the camps made that impossible — but the freedom to decide what the circumstances mean, and what response to them best expresses the values and purposes by which one has chosen to live.

Applied to the Worth Paradox: the fact that an AI can perform your professional tasks does not determine what meaning you attach to your professional activity, or what purposes you pursue through it, or what kind of person you become in the process of engaging with it. These are questions that remain, in Frankl's sense, in the space between the stimulus of technological disruption and your response to it. They are questions that only you can answer. And the way you answer them will determine not whether you are useful in the market's sense, but whether you are living in a way that reflects your deepest values and fullest humanity.

BUDDHIST NON-ATTACHMENT AND THE PROBLEM OF CLINGING

The Buddhist tradition offers yet another angle on the Worth Paradox, one that is particularly illuminating when considered alongside the psychological literature on contingent self-worth. The Buddhist concept of upadana — often translated as 'clinging' or 'attachment' — describes the habitual tendency to grasp at things, experiences, and identities as if they could provide permanent refuge from the fundamental impermanence of existence.

In Buddhist psychology, suffering arises not from impermanence itself — everything is impermanent, and that is simply the nature of existence — but from the refusal to accept impermanence; from the grasping after permanence in things that cannot provide it. The person who has built their identity around their professional role and its market value has, in Buddhist terms, clung to an identity that was always impermanent. The disruption that AI represents is not creating the impermanence — it is simply making visible an impermanence that was always there.

This perspective does not trivialize the pain of displacement. It contextualizes it. The pain is real, and it deserves to be taken seriously. But it is, in part, the pain of impermanence — the pain that arises whenever we discover that something we had taken to be a stable foundation was, like everything else, subject to change. The Buddhist response to this pain is not to find a more durable foundation in the same domain but to investigate the nature of identity itself — to ask whether the self that is clinging to the professional identity is as solid and fixed as the clinging assumes.

VII. Result-Oriented vs. Process-Oriented Living

One of the most useful frameworks for understanding the Worth Paradox — and for navigating the path toward its resolution — is the distinction between Result-Oriented Living and Process-Oriented Living.

Result-Oriented Living is the mode of existence that the Church of the Grind both produces and requires. In this mode, the value of any activity is determined entirely by its output: the finished report, the closed deal, the completed project, the achieved metric. The activity itself is merely a means to the result. This is precisely the logic by which AI threatens the value of human cognitive labor: if the output is what matters, and an AI can produce a better output faster and more cheaply, then the human activity has been surpassed.

Process-Oriented Living operates on an entirely different logic. In this mode, the value of an activity resides not in its output but in the quality of engagement the activity calls forth: the depth of attention it requires, the challenges it poses, the ways it develops capacity in meeting them, the connections it forges between people and between a person and their own interior life. The value in Process-Oriented Living is not in the destination but in the struggle and growth of the journey. And this is a value that artificial intelligence cannot absorb because it does not reside in the output at all. It resides in the human being who engaged with the process. It is, in the deepest sense, irreducibly personal.

The Practice of Process-Orientation

The shift from result-oriented to process-oriented living is not achieved by an act of will. It is a practice — a set of habits of attention and engagement that are cultivated gradually, over time, against the powerful gravitational pull of a culture that rewards results and ignores process. Several practices have proven particularly useful.

The first is what we might call the cultivation of genuine curiosity. Curiosity — not the performed curiosity of someone who wants to appear interested, but the real thing, the kind that pulls you into a subject and makes you forget to check your metrics — is the signature emotion of process-oriented engagement. It is also, not coincidentally, the emotion that AI systems most spectacularly lack. A language model can produce text that sounds curious. It experiences nothing. The human being who is genuinely curious about a problem, who follows the problem into unexpected territory and discovers connections that no one had anticipated, is doing something that is both intrinsically valuable and, at least for now, genuinely rare.

The second practice is the deliberate cultivation of what psychologist Mihaly Csikszentmihalyi called 'flow' — the state of absorbed, effortful engagement in which the gap between challenge and capacity is optimal: large enough to demand full attention and small enough to permit genuine achievement. Flow states are among the most reliable sources of intrinsic meaning available to human beings. They are also, by their nature, process-oriented: in flow, you are not thinking about the output. You are entirely inside the activity.

The third practice is the cultivation of genuine relationship in professional contexts — the kind of connection that goes beyond the transactional exchange of professional outputs and engages the full human beings on both sides of the interaction. The human dimension of work — the mentoring, the collaboration, the shared problem-solving that emerges from genuine mutual trust and respect — is not merely a pleasant addition to the real work. For many people, and in many contexts, it is the real work. And it is, by its nature, irreplaceable.

VIII. The New Metrics of a Worthwhile Life

If the old metric of worth — market value of outputs — is inadequate to the moment we are living through, we need new metrics. Not as a consolation prize for those who have lost the old competition, but as a more accurate and philosophically defensible account of what makes a human life genuinely worthwhile.

The following framework is offered not as a prescription but as a starting point for the kind of personal reflection that the Worth Paradox demands. Different people will weight these dimensions differently, and the process of working out one's own weighting is itself a significant part of the work.

Depth of Engagement

The first dimension of a worthwhile life is the quality of attention and engagement you bring to the activities that constitute it. A life in which you are genuinely present — absorbed, challenged, curious, alive to the texture of your experience — is a worthwhile life regardless of what it produces. This is not mysticism; it is basic phenomenology. The experience of full engagement is intrinsically valuable, and no technological development can make it less so.

Quality of Relationship

The second dimension is the depth and quality of your connections with other people. The research on human flourishing is unambiguous on this point: across cultures, across income levels, across historical periods, the single most reliable predictor of subjective well-being is the quality of one's close relationships. Not career achievement. Not wealth. Not status. Relationships. A life rich in genuine connection — characterized by mutual care, honest communication, and the quality of presence that comes from being fully known and fully knowing another — is a worthwhile life. Full stop.

Contribution Beyond Transaction

The third dimension is contribution — not the transactional contribution that the market measures and rewards, but the kind that is given freely and received personally. The parent who reads to their child is contributing something that no AI will ever replicate, not because the story is better when read by a parent than when delivered by a machine, but because the child who is held and read to is receiving not just a story but the embodied presence of someone who loves them. The volunteer who sits with an elderly person in a hospital is contributing something that cannot be captured in any output metric. The friend who shows up at 2 a.m. when you are in crisis is contributing something that has no market value and infinite human value.

Growth and the Edges of Capacity

The fourth dimension is growth — the ongoing expansion of your capacity to engage with, understand, and respond to the world. This is not the performative growth of the self-improvement industry, which tends to reduce development to a series of optimizations. It is the genuine growth that comes from taking on challenges that exceed your current capacity, failing, learning, and trying again. The human being who is genuinely growing — who is regularly operating at the edges of what they can do, in service of something they genuinely care about — is living a worthwhile life. The outputs they produce along the way are, in this perspective, secondary evidence of the growth itself.

> *The question to ask yourself is not 'What have I produced?' but 'What kind of person am I becoming, and is that person someone I recognize and respect?'*

IX. A Letter to the Person in the Middle of It

If you are reading this chapter and it is speaking to something real in your experience — if you recognize yourself in the portraits of Uselessness Syndrome, or in the description of the shame economy, or in the account of how deeply the ideology of meritocracy has embedded itself in your sense of who you are — then this last section is addressed directly to you.

First: what you are feeling is not weakness. It is not a character flaw. It is not evidence that you are failing to adapt or that you lack resilience. It is the entirely rational response of a human being whose sense of worth has been built on a foundation that is shifting beneath their feet. The fact that you feel it means you are paying attention. The people who are not feeling anything are not managing better. They are, in many cases, managing worse — they have simply found more effective ways of not looking.

Second: the disruption is real, and the anxiety is legitimate. There is no point in pretending otherwise. AI is genuinely transforming the nature of cognitive work, and the transformation will require real adaptation — new skills, new orientations, new ways of thinking about what it means to contribute. The process of that adaptation is, for most people, neither quick nor painless. To acknowledge this is not to be pessimistic. It is to be honest about the scale of the challenge.

Third: you are more than what you produce. I do not mean this as a reassurance or a platitude. I mean it as a straightforward factual claim about the nature of human worth that has been obscured by two centuries of productivity ideology and that the current moment is forcing us, with unusual urgency, to recover. You were a person of full and unconditional worth before you had a job title. You will be a person of full and unconditional worth when that job title has been transformed beyond recognition. The market's assessment of your utility is information about the market. It is not a verdict about you.

Fourth: the path forward is not primarily a path of optimization. It is a path of reorientation. The question is not 'How do I make myself more competitive in a world of AI?' — though practical adaptation matters and should not be dismissed. The deeper question is: 'Given that the world is changing in ways I cannot fully control, what kind of life do I want to be building? What do I genuinely value beyond the productivity metrics by which I have been measuring myself? What would it mean to do excellent work — not just work that produces valued outputs, but work that expresses my values, develops my capacity, serves the people I care about, and makes me someone I recognize in the mirror?'

These are not easy questions. They are, in fact, among the hardest questions a human being can ask, because they require a kind of honesty about what matters that the busyness of a productive life makes it easy to avoid. But they are the right questions. And the fact that the current technological moment is forcing them onto the agenda with such urgency may, eventually, turn out to be its most important gift.

The Worth Paradox is not a paradox about technology. It is a paradox about identity — about the stories we tell ourselves about who we are and what makes us valuable. The resolution of the paradox is not a technological solution or an

economic policy. It is a personal reckoning: a willingness to question the foundations on which the sense of self has been built, and to begin the work of rebuilding on ground that is more durable, more honest, and more fully human.

CHAPTER FIVE

THE DOPAMINE TRAP

✦ ✦ ✦

I. THE VOID AND WHAT RUSHES TO FILL IT

There is a specific quality of emptiness that descends in the aftermath of loss. Not the sharp, clarifying pain of acute grief, which at least has the virtue of intensity and direction, but the duller, more disorienting emptiness that follows the slow erosion of something that once gave a life its structure and forward momentum. The loss of a marriage that had long been over before it ended. The departure of children from a house that had been organized around their presence for twenty years. The retirement from a career that, whatever its frustrations, had provided a reliable skeleton of purpose around which each day was organized. These losses share a particular phenomenological quality: the sudden, vertiginous awareness of unstructured time, of a self with no designated function, of a day that does not know what it is for.

The Identity Crash produces exactly this quality of emptiness, but with a distinctive additional dimension that the other losses do not carry. The retired professional, the empty-nesting parent, the recently divorced person: these individuals have lost something specific, something nameable, something whose absence is socially recognized and for which social rituals of transition have been, however inadequately, developed. The person whose professional identity has been eroded by the Efficiency Wall loses something that cannot be named without triggering either denial or defensiveness, grieves something that has no funeral, and confronts an unstructured time that arrives not after a recognized life transition but in the middle of what is nominally still a fully functioning professional life.

Into this specific quality of emptiness — the purposeless surplus time of the Identity Crash, arriving without social recognition, without legitimate vocabulary, and without the conventional support structures of recognized transition — something rushes with extraordinary speed, extraordinary efficiency, and extraordinary sophistication. It is not a person. It is not a community. It is not a practice, a discipline, or a wisdom tradition. It is a system: the algorithmically optimized, perpetually available, hyper-personalized digital attention economy that has been constructed over the past two decades, with the explicit purpose of capturing and holding human attention as effectively as possible for as long as possible.

The Dopamine Trap is the name for what happens at the intersection of these two forces: the specific psychological vulnerability created by the Identity Crash, and the specific capabilities of the attention economy designed to exploit exactly that kind of vulnerability. It is a trap not because it is entered through malice or stupidity, but because it is entered through the entirely reasonable human impulse to find relief from a form of suffering that has no other immediately available remedy. And it is a trap because the relief it offers — real, immediate, and temporarily effective — is purchased at a cost that is invisible in the moment of purchase and paid, with compound interest, over months and years of progressive psychological and cognitive impoverishment.

Understanding the trap — its mechanisms, its costs, and the specific conditions that make it so difficult to exit once entered — is the necessary precondition for finding a genuine alternative. This chapter is that understanding.

II. A Brief History of Manufactured Desire

The manufacture of desire — the deliberate engineering of human wanting in the service of commercial or political objectives — is not a new phenomenon. Its modern form was inaugurated by Edward Bernays, the nephew of Sigmund Freud, whose 1928 book Propaganda described with cheerful frankness the techniques by which the insights of psychoanalysis could be applied to the management of public behavior on behalf of corporate clients. Bernays was not the first person to recognize that human beings could be influenced by appealing to their unconscious drives rather than their rational interests. He was the first to systematize the insight and sell it as a professional service.

The advertising industry that emerged from Bernays's pioneering work spent most of the twentieth century developing and refining the techniques of desire manufacture: the association of products with aspirational identities, the exploitation of anxiety and insecurity, the creation of social norms that defined adequacy in ways that could only be met through consumption. By the mid-twentieth century, the manufactured desire industry had become one of the most sophisticated psychological influence operations in human history, backed by substantial research budgets and the collective intelligence of some of the most talented communicators, artists, and psychologists of the era.

And yet, by the standards of what was to come, the twentieth-century advertising industry was operating with extraordinarily blunt instruments. Its reach was limited by the distribution channels available to it: newspapers, radio, television, billboards, and the postal service. Its personalization was zero: the same advertisement reached every viewer of a given program, regardless of their individual psychological profile, their specific vulnerabilities, or their susceptibility to specific forms of appeal. Its feedback loops were slow and indirect: months passed between the deployment of a campaign and the arrival of sales data that might indicate whether it was working.

The digital revolution, and specifically the emergence of the algorithmically personalized social media platform in the first decade of the twenty-first century, transformed every one of these limitations simultaneously. Distribution became universal: the smartphone in every pocket provided access to every person, at every moment, in every location. Personalization became extraordinary: the behavioral data generated by billions of users interacting with digital platforms provided a training dataset for recommendation and content-delivery algorithms of previously unimaginable sophistication. And feedback loops became instantaneous: the response of each user to each piece of content was available in real time, allowing continuous refinement of the algorithms in the direction of maximum engagement.

The result was not merely a more effective advertising industry. It was, in effect, a new kind of relationship between human psychology and technological system: one in which the system had access to more information about each individual's psychological state, preferences, vulnerabilities, and behavioral patterns than the individual themselves typically possessed, and in which that information was deployed continuously and in real time to shape the individual's attention, mood, and behavior in directions that maximized the system's commercial objectives. The attention economy, in its mature form, is not a media business. It is a psychological infrastructure — one that has been built, with extraordinary care and extraordinary resources, specifically around the features of human psychology that make it most susceptible to capture and manipulation.

III. The Neuroscience of the Trap: Dopamine, Prediction, and the Slot Machine

To understand why the digital attention economy is so effective at what it does — and why it is so specifically dangerous in the context of the Identity Crash — it is necessary to understand something about the neuroscience of the brain systems it has been engineered to exploit. The relevant system is the mesolimbic dopamine pathway: a set of neural circuits connecting the ventral tegmental area of the midbrain to the nucleus accumbens and prefrontal cortex, which plays a vital role in motivation, reward-seeking, and the subjective experience of wanting.

The popular understanding of dopamine — as the "pleasure chemical," the neurotransmitter of enjoyment and satisfaction — is a significant oversimplification of what the neuroscience shows. The more accurate picture, developed through decades of research by neuroscientists including Wolfram Schultz, Kent Berridge, and Terry Robinson, is more interesting and more relevant to the Dopamine Trap. Dopamine is not primarily the chemical of pleasure. It is primarily the chemical of anticipation: of the expectation of reward, the prediction of something good about to arrive, the mobilization of attention and behavior in the direction of a potential positive outcome.

This distinction matters enormously. The dopamine system is not activated by receiving a reward. It is activated by the prediction of a reward — specifically, by the gap between the predicted probability of reward and the actual delivery. When a reward arrives that was predicted with certainty, the dopamine response is minimal: the brain already knew this was coming, and there is no added information to process. When a reward arrives that was not predicted — a surprise positive outcome — the dopamine response is large. And when an expected reward fails to arrive — a prediction error in the negative direction — dopamine activity drops below baseline: a signal of disappointment that motivates the system to update its predictions and adjust its behavior.

The implications of this architecture for the design of maximally engaging digital experiences were understood, explicitly or implicitly, by the engineers of the first generation of social media platforms and have been systematically refined ever since. The most addictive digital experiences are not those that deliver consistent, high-quality rewards. They are those that deliver rewards intermittently and unpredictably — that create a pattern of engagement in which the user cannot know in advance whether the next scroll, the next notification, the next post will contain something important, entertaining, or validating, but where the possibility that it might is sufficient to sustain continued engagement.

This is precisely the architecture of the slot machine, which behavioral psychologists have known for decades to be the most addictive form of gambling. The slot machine does not pay out on every pull. It pays out on a variable ratio schedule: sometimes after one pull, sometimes after a hundred, with no pattern the player can predict or exploit. This unpredictability is not a design flaw. It is the core design feature. The variable ratio schedule produces the highest and most persistent rates of reward-seeking behavior of any reinforcement schedule because the dopamine system never fully extinguishes the hope of the next reward and never fully habituates to the pattern of delivery.

The infinite scroll, the notification badge, the algorithmic feed, the like counter — these are all variable ratio schedules. They are slot machines optimized through billions of interactions with human users to deliver the precise pattern of intermittent, unpredictable reward that maximizes dopamine-driven engagement. The people who built them did not necessarily set out to create addictive products. Many of them set out to build useful communication tools, entertainment platforms, or information services. But the competitive pressures of the attention economy — in which advertising revenue is directly proportional to engagement metrics — created systematic incentives to optimize for the features of the product that most effectively captured and held attention, regardless of whether those features were good for the people using them.

The result is a digital environment that has been, in effect, tuned to the specific frequencies of human psychological vulnerability with a precision that no previous technology has approached. It is not merely persuasive. It is, in the technical sense of the term, addictive: it creates patterns of compulsive use that persist in the face of the user's own stated preferences and intentions, that are associated with withdrawal-like discomfort when access is interrupted, and that progressively crowd out other activities and experiences that would, in a more balanced psychological ecology, serve the user's genuine long-term interests.

IV. The Identity Crash as Vulnerability: Why the Trap Is Deeper Now

The digital attention economy has been operating as a significant psychological hazard for a decade and a half. Its effects on attention, mood, social comparison, and mental health have been extensively documented in both the research literature and the broader cultural conversation. For many people, even before the Identity Crash began in earnest, the relationship with social media and digital entertainment had already become problematic: a source of distraction, anxiety, and progressive erosion of the capacity for sustained, self-directed engagement.

But the Identity Crash changes the parameters of this relationship in ways that are qualitatively, not merely quantitatively, significant. It does so by altering the specific psychological conditions under which each individual encounters the attention economy — and specifically, by creating a set of conditions that are precisely those under which the trap is most effective and most dangerous.

The trap is most effective when three specific conditions are simultaneously present. The first is an acute deficit of felt purpose: a state in which the activities that previously gave the day its structure and the self its sense of direction are no longer performing that function, leaving behind a psychological vacuum that the motivational system experiences as urgently in need of filling. The second is an availability of unstructured time: the physical space and temporal freedom that the absence of genuine cognitive demands creates, which provides the opportunity for extended digital engagement that would not exist in a schedule fully occupied by genuinely demanding activities. The third is the absence of immediately available, equally accessible alternatives: the condition in which the most readily available source of stimulation, engagement, and temporary relief from the discomfort of purposelessness is the digital environment, rather than physical community, embodied activity, or the slow satisfactions of genuine creative work.

The Identity Crash creates all three of these conditions simultaneously and reliably. The erosion of professional identity removes the primary source of felt purpose for most knowledge workers. The automation of cognitive tasks creates genuine surpluses of unstructured time. And the dissolution of the professional community and daily social infrastructure that organized work provided — the colleagues, the routines, the shared context — removes the most readily available alternatives to digital engagement that might otherwise compete with it.

This is why the Dopamine Trap is not merely a background feature of the Identity Crash but one of its primary active dangers. In the absence of the conditions that make genuine resistance to the trap possible — felt purpose, structured time, accessible community — the pull of the digital attention economy on the psychologically vulnerable person is not a matter of weak willpower or insufficient discipline. It is a predictable, almost inevitable response of a human nervous system to a specific set of environmental conditions. The trap does not require personal failure to spring. It requires only the presence of the conditions that the Identity Crash reliably creates.

V. Digital Opium: The Pharmacology of Scrolling

The comparison between digital engagement and opiate use is not merely rhetorical provocation. It reflects a genuine and increasingly well-documented set of neurobiological parallels that are worth examining in some detail, because they illuminate both why the Dopamine Trap is so difficult to exit and what genuine exit requires.

Opiates produce their characteristic effects — euphoria, pain relief, anxiolysis, and the suppression of negative affect — by binding to the mu-opioid receptors that are distributed throughout the brain and peripheral nervous system. These receptors are part of a system that evolved to regulate the experience of pain and reward in the context of biologically noteworthy events: the endorphin release that accompanies vigorous exercise, the opioid activity associated with social bonding and attachment, the natural analgesia that moderates the experience of physical injury. The opiate drugs hijack this system by delivering an exogenous signal of far greater intensity than the natural system can produce, overwhelming the regulatory mechanisms that would normally keep the system in balance.

The behavioral consequences of this hijacking are well known. The user experiences an initial period of relief, euphoria, or pleasant sedation that is real and genuinely pleasurable. But the brain's homeostatic mechanisms respond to the abnormally high opioid signal by downregulating receptor sensitivity: reducing the number and responsiveness of mu-opioid receptors to restore equilibrium. The result is tolerance — the requirement for progressively larger doses to achieve the same effect — and, eventually, a baseline state that is not merely neutral but genuinely aversive: the withdrawal syndrome that occurs when the exogenous opioid signal is removed and the downregulated natural system is insufficient to maintain normal function.

The digital attention economy produces a functionally analogous process through a different neurochemical pathway. The variable-ratio reward schedules of social media and digital entertainment produce chronic, low-grade dopamine stimulation that, over time, alters the sensitivity and responsiveness of the mesolimbic reward system. The baseline level of stimulation that the system comes to expect — and to require for normal psychological functioning — is progressively elevated. The activities that previously generated adequate dopaminergic reward — reading, conversation, physical activity, creative work, quiet reflection — become subjectively less satisfying because they generate lower dopamine responses than the system has been calibrated to expect. The pull toward the digital environment intensifies not because the environment becomes more rewarding but because the non-digital environment becomes, by comparison, progressively more aversive.

This is the pharmacological logic of the trap. It is not a metaphor. It is a description of a genuine neurobiological process that is occurring in real time, in millions of people, and that has measurable consequences for the capacity for sustained attention, genuine emotional engagement, and the deep, slow satisfactions of genuinely demanding activity that constitute the substance of a meaningful life. The person who has spent years in heavy engagement with the digital attention economy does not merely lack the habit of deep engagement. They have a nervous system that has been calibrated, through repeated and sustained stimulation, to find deep engagement less rewarding than it would otherwise be — and to find its absence more uncomfortable than a nervous system that had not undergone this calibration would find it.

This is a genuinely serious observation, and it deserves a genuinely serious response. Not panic, and not the moralistic condemnation of digital technology as inherently evil. But clear-eyed acknowledgment that the engagement patterns produced by the Dopamine Trap are not merely habits that can be changed through an act of will. They are neurobiological states that require a genuine process of recalibration — a process that takes time, that involves real discomfort, and that requires the development of genuine alternatives rather than merely the subtraction of the problematic behavior.

VI. The Feedback Loop of Sedation and Shame

The Dopamine Trap would be dangerous enough if its effects were simply the erosion of attention and the progressive impoverishment of the capacity for genuine engagement. But the trap has a second component that makes it significantly more damaging than this description suggests: the feedback loop of sedation and shame that amplifies and entrenches the initial pattern of digital escape, making it progressively harder to exit with each iteration of the cycle.

The loop works as follows. The person in the grip of the Identity Crash — experiencing the specific combination of purposelessness, unstructured time, and absence of community that makes them maximally vulnerable to the trap — turns to digital stimulation for relief. The relief is real. In the short term, the engagement of the dopamine system by the variable-ratio rewards of social media, streaming content, or algorithmically curated entertainment genuinely reduces the subjective discomfort of purposelessness. The scroll provides stimulation where there was emptiness. The notification provides a sense of connection where there was isolation. The algorithmic content stream provides a sense of engagement where there was boredom. These are not trivial benefits. They are genuine, if temporary, ameliorations of genuine suffering.

The problem arrives on the return to baseline. After the session of digital engagement ends — whether by deliberate choice or by the depletion of the stimulation's effectiveness as tolerance increases — the person does not return to the same psychological state they inhabited before the session began. They return to a state that is, typically, worse: a state that includes not only the original purposelessness and emptiness but an additional layer of negative affect generated by the recognition of what just occurred. The hour spent scrolling did not address the underlying condition. It did not produce any genuine progress toward the resolution of the Identity Crash. It did not build any of the capabilities, relationships, or practices that the post-Efficiency Wall world requires. It consumed time and attention that might have been invested in something genuinely restorative, and it leaves behind, for most people who are honest with themselves, a residue of self-reproach.

This self-reproach is the shame component of the loop. It is, importantly, not a product of moral weakness or excessive self-criticism. It is an accurate recognition, at some level of psychological processing, that the activity engaged in was not serving one's genuine interests. The shame is information: a signal from the self-evaluating mind that there is a discrepancy between one's values and one's behavior. In a context where that signal could be heard and acted upon — where the person had the psychological resources, the genuine alternatives, and the social support to respond to the signal constructively — it would be adaptive. It would prompt behavioral change in the direction of the values it is registering as violated.

But in the context of the Identity Crash, the shame signal typically cannot be acted upon constructively, because the conditions that produced the digital escape in the first place — the purposelessness, the isolation, the absence of immediately available alternatives — remain in place. The shame deepens the discomfort. The deepened discomfort intensifies the craving for relief. The relief is most immediately available in the digital environment. The next session of digital engagement begins. And the shame that follows it is, typically, deeper than the shame that followed the last one, because the pattern is now more clearly established, the self-knowledge more uncomfortable, and the gap between aspiration and behavior more difficult to explain away.

Over time, this loop produces a progressive erosion of the self-concept that is, in the context of the Identity Crash, extremely dangerous. The person who entered the trap already suffering from a damaged sense of professional worth exits it, gradually and incrementally, with a damaged sense of personal worth as well: a sense of being someone who cannot maintain their own standards, who reaches for distraction rather than engaging with difficulty, who is being managed by a commercial system rather than managing their own attention and time. This additional layer of self-diminishment compounds the original damage of the Identity Crash in ways that make genuine recovery significantly more difficult.

VII. The AI Amplification: When the Trap Gets Smarter

The Dopamine Trap as described in the preceding sections is already, by any reasonable assessment, a serious and widespread problem. But it is a problem that has been operating, until recently, with what are, in retrospect, primitive tools. The recommendation algorithms of the first generation of social media platforms — sophisticated as they were compared to anything that preceded them — were working with coarse models of user psychology: behavioral data about past engagement, demographic proxies for preference, and the aggregate patterns of users with similar histories. They were powerful. They were not, in the full sense of the word, intelligent.

The application of genuinely capable AI to the attention economy — a development that is already well underway and accelerating — is not merely an incremental improvement in the sophistication of existing systems. It represents a qualitative transformation in the nature of the trap. Where the previous generation of recommendation systems worked with behavioral proxies and statistical correlations, the emerging generation works with something much closer to genuine psychological modeling: real-time assessment of the individual user's emotional state, cognitive condition, and specific susceptibilities, derived from a combination of behavioral signals, linguistic analysis, temporal patterns of engagement, and the increasingly rich biometric data available from wearable devices and the cameras and microphones of ubiquitous smartphones.

This is not speculation. The capacity to infer emotional state from behavioral signals — typing speed, scrolling velocity, facial expression, vocal characteristics — is already commercially deployed in multiple contexts, including the optimization of digital content delivery. The capacity to model individual psychological vulnerability in real time and adjust content delivery accordingly is the logical and commercially obvious extension of capabilities that already exist in less refined forms. The question is not whether this capacity will be developed. It is whether the people who are being subjected to it will develop the understanding and the practices necessary to resist it effectively.

The AI-augmented Dopamine Trap does not merely serve content that the user is likely to engage with. It serves content that the user is, at this specific moment, in this specific psychological state, least able to resist: content calibrated not to their stable preferences but to their current vulnerabilities. The person who is experiencing the specific combination of purposelessness, loneliness, and self-doubt that characterizes the acute phase of the Identity Crash is, for the AI-augmented attention economy, not merely a user with certain engagement preferences. They are a profile with specific exploitable features: the content that will most effectively capture their attention, hold it longest, and bring them back soonest is derivable, with increasing accuracy, from the real-time analysis of their psychological state.

This represents an asymmetry of capability that is, in some ways, the attention economy's own Efficiency Wall: the same exponential improvement in AI capability that is disrupting professional cognitive labor is also being deployed, with equally exponential sophistication, against the psychological defenses of the human beings whose cognitive labor it is displacing. The person navigating the Identity Crash is simultaneously losing their professional cognitive advantage to AI and finding their psychological defenses against AI-optimized manipulation progressively eroded. The trap becomes smarter precisely as the person it is targeting becomes more vulnerable.

This observation is not intended to produce despair. But it is intended to produce clarity about the genuine nature of what is being navigated. The Dopamine Trap is not a simple habit problem. It is not a matter of insufficient willpower or insufficient self-awareness. It is an encounter between a human nervous system in a specific state of vulnerability and a technological system of extraordinary sophistication that has been specifically optimized to exploit that vulnerability. The appropriate response is not self-blame but strategy: the deliberate, informed construction of a personal environment and a personal practice that reduces vulnerability, provides genuine alternatives, and develops the psychological capacities that make genuine resistance possible.

VIII. The Default Mode Network and the Value of Unstructured Mind

Against the backdrop of the Dopamine Trap's seductive efficiency, the practice of simply sitting with an unoccupied mind can seem not merely unappealing but almost irrational. Why tolerate the discomfort of unstimulated consciousness when an algorithm stands ready to fill every available moment with content calibrated to your specific preferences? What could unstructured, undirected mental time offer that the attention economy's infinite library of optimized engagement cannot?

The answer, as neuroscience has increasingly revealed, is both surprising and profound. The brain in a state of undirected rest — the state that we experience subjectively as mind-wandering, daydreaming, or simply being bored — is not in a state of reduced activity. It is in a state of reorganized activity: a mode of neural processing that is different from, and in important respects complementary to, the directed, goal-focused processing of intentional cognitive work.

The neural network most associated with this mode of processing is called the default mode network: a set of brain regions — including the medial prefrontal cortex, the posterior cingulate cortex, and the angular gyrus — that are consistently active during rest and consistently deactivated during focused external attention. The default mode network was initially understood, when it was first characterized in the late 1990s and early 2000s, primarily as a baseline state: the brain's idling condition, active only in the absence of more demanding cognitive tasks. Subsequent research has revealed a more interesting picture.

The default mode network is now understood to be the primary neural substrate of a set of cognitive functions that are among the most distinctively human and most important for psychological wellbeing and creative capacity. These functions include autobiographical memory consolidation — the process by which episodic experiences are integrated into coherent long-term narratives of the self. They include mental time travel — the simulation of past scenarios and the imaginative projection into future ones that underlies both learning from experience and planning for the future. They include perspective-taking — the imaginative inhabitation of other minds and the modeling of other people's mental states that forms the neural basis of empathy. And they include the kind of associative, non-linear thinking that produces creative insight: the unexpected connection between unrelated ideas, the novel solution to an intractable problem, the sudden reorganization of existing knowledge into a new and more revealing framework.

All these functions require the default mode network to operate without interruption from external demands on attention. They are, by their nature, slow processes: they require time, quiet, and the absence of the constant attentional redirection that the digital environment provides. The mind that is perpetually stimulated by external content — that is never allowed to idle, never allowed to wander, never allowed to follow its own associative threads wherever they might lead — is a mind that is being systematically deprived of the conditions under which its most important work occurs.

The Dopamine Trap, in this neurological context, is not merely a distraction from more valuable activities. It is an active suppression of a specific set of cognitive processes that are essential to psychological integration, creative capacity, and the development of the kind of self-knowledge that genuine adaptation to the Identity Crash requires. Every hour spent in the algorithmically managed stimulation of the digital environment is an hour in which the default mode network — the brain's meaning-making, self-integrating, creativity-generating operating system — is offline. The cumulative effect of years of heavy digital engagement is not merely a distracted mind. It is a mind that has progressively lost the capacity for the specific kind of processing that would allow it to genuinely understand its own situation and genuinely imagine its way toward something better.

IX. The Discipline of Boredom: Reclaiming the Unoccupied Mind

The Discipline of Boredom is a deliberately paradoxical formulation. Boredom, in the contemporary cultural imagination, is something to be eliminated: a problem to be solved, a discomfort to be relieved, an empty space to be filled. The suggestion that boredom might be something to be cultivated — approached with discipline, practiced with intention, and valued as a resource rather than tolerated as a deprivation — runs directly against the grain of the attention economy's entire value proposition and the centuries of cultural conditioning that preceded it.

And yet the research on boredom, creativity, and psychological wellbeing increasingly supports this counterintuitive position. Studies by Sandi Mann and Rebekah Cadman at the University of Central Lancashire found that participants who were deliberately bored before performing a creative task — by being asked to copy numbers from a telephone directory for an extended period — generated significantly more creative ideas in the subsequent task than participants who had not been bored. The explanation offered was consistent with what we know about the default mode network: the period of enforced, under stimulated inactivity allowed the mind to enter the associative, generative mode of processing that produces creative insight, whereas the directly stimulated comparison group arrived at the creative task with their attentional systems already committed to the patterns established by the prior stimulating activity.

The Discipline of Boredom, as a practice, begins with something deceptively simple: the deliberate creation of regular periods of time in which no external stimulation is sought or permitted. Not meditation, necessarily — though meditation is one form this practice can take. Not journaling, not walking while listening to a podcast, not reading while eating. Simply: time in which the mind is given nothing to do and allowed to do whatever it chooses with that freedom. Time in which the discomfort of unstimulated consciousness is neither fled from nor analyzed, but simply inhabited, as one might inhabit a difficult posture in a physical practice: with attention, with patience, and with the understanding that the discomfort is not a signal to stop but a signal that something genuine and important is happening.

The initial experience of this practice, for most people who have been heavily engaged with the digital attention economy, is genuinely uncomfortable. The attentional system, trained through years of variable-ratio reward to orient toward external stimulation, experiences its absence as aversive: a craving, a restlessness, a pervasive sense that something important might be being missed and that relief is only a reach toward the phone away. This is the withdrawal dimension of the Dopamine Trap, and it is real. The discomfort is not imaginary. It is the felt experience of a nervous system that has been calibrated to expect a level of stimulation that is not currently being provided.

But the discomfort is survivable. And on the other side of it — typically after ten to twenty minutes of genuine tolerance of the unstimulated state — something begins to shift. The attentional system, finding no external target to orient toward, turns inward. The default mode network activates. Thoughts arrive that were not deliberately summoned: memories, associations, half-formed ideas, the beginnings of connections between things that had previously seemed unrelated. The quality of mental experience changes from the agitated emptiness of the early minutes to something quieter, less urgent, and genuinely interesting — the specific quality of interest that arises when one's own mind is allowed to show you what it has been thinking about when you weren't paying attention.

This is not a minor or optional benefit. For the person navigating the Identity Crash — who needs, more urgently than anything else, a genuine encounter with the dimensions of their own experience, values, and capacities that the Church of the Grind has suppressed and the Dopamine Trap is actively preventing from surfacing — the practice of the Discipline of Boredom is one of the most important cognitive and psychological investments available. It is the practice of making space for the self that exists beneath the performance of the self — the self that knows things the professional persona does not know, that wants things the resume does not mention, and that has a genuine sense of direction that no algorithm can provide.

X. Friction as Feature: Redesigning the Personal Environment

The Discipline of Boredom is a practice of internal recalibration: the deliberate retraining of the attentional and reward systems toward deeper, slower, less immediately stimulating but more genuinely nourishing forms of engagement. But internal recalibration, however important, is insufficient on its own. The neurobiological research on behavior change is consistent on this point: changing patterns of behavior that are sustained by powerful environmental cues requires not only internal motivation but environmental redesign. The person who attempts to change their relationship with the digital attention economy through willpower alone, in an environment that remains unchanged, is attempting to swim upstream against a current that has been specifically engineered to be stronger than willpower.

The concept of "friction as feature" describes the deliberate introduction of physical, temporal, or cognitive obstacles between the person and the behaviors associated with the Dopamine Trap — not as a punitive measure, but as an environmental design strategy that reduces the automaticity of digital engagement and creates space for deliberate choice. Every moment of friction in the path between an impulse and its digital gratification is a moment in which the reflective system could intervene: to notice the impulse, consider its origins, and decide whether acting on it serves one's genuine interests.

The practical applications of this principle are simple, well-documented, and genuinely effective. Removing social media applications from the phone rather than merely turning off notifications. Placing the phone in another room during the hours designated for analog engagement. Using a physical alarm clock rather than a phone alarm, to break the morning ritual of device-first consciousness. Designating specific physical locations — a desk, a reading chair, a kitchen table — as screen-free zones associated with the activities that the Dopamine Trap is crowding out. These are not high-technology solutions. They are environmental design interventions that work by increasing the behavioral cost of digital escape and decreasing the behavioral cost of genuine engagement.

The complementary principle is the deliberate introduction of genuinely friction-rich alternatives to digital engagement: activities that are demanding, slow, physically involving, and resistant to the kind of frictionless consumption that the attention economy provides. The physical book that cannot be hyperlinked, algorithmically recommended, or interrupted by a notification. The craft that requires sustained attention to a physical material and produces visible evidence of genuine human effort. The conversation that must be navigated in real time, without the mediation of a screen, with the full demand of another person's presence. The exercise that requires physical exertion and tolerates no distraction. These activities do not substitute for digital engagement. They actively rebuild the capacities that digital engagement erodes: the capacity for sustained attention, for genuine presence, for the slow, effortful, and deeply satisfying form of engagement that produces genuine growth rather than merely pleasant stimulation.

The broader reorientation that the concept of friction as feature points toward is one of the most important cognitive shifts available to the person navigating the Identity Crash: the shift from evaluating activities primarily by their ease and immediate pleasure to evaluating them by their contribution to genuine flourishing. The activities that are easiest — that offer the least resistance, the most immediate gratification, the lowest barrier to entry — are, in the current environment, almost by definition the activities that the attention economy has engineered to be that way. Ease, in this context, is not a neutral feature. It is a design specification in the service of commercial objectives that are not aligned with the user's genuine interests.

Difficulty, by contrast — the friction of a demanding book, the resistance of a physical craft, the challenge of a genuine conversation, the discomfort of an unoccupied mind — is, in the current environment, almost by definition the territory of genuine human value. It is the territory that the attention economy cannot commoditize, cannot automate, and cannot provide. It is, in the deepest sense of the term, the territory of the self that is trying to survive the Identity Crash and emerge, on the other side of it, as something more genuinely alive than the productive unit the Church of the Grind had trained it to be.

The trap is not the destination. It is the detour. And the door out has always been open.

CHAPTER SIX

THE HUMAN RENAISSANCE

I. THE PATTERN OF CIVILIZATIONAL CRISIS

History does not repeat itself. But it does, with sufficient regularity to warrant the observation, rhyme. And among the most consistent rhymes in the historical record is this one: that the greatest periods of human creative and cultural flourishing have emerged not from conditions of stability and comfort, but from the wreckage of collapsed certainty. The moments when the old frameworks have dissolved, the old hierarchies have crumbled, and the old answers have been revealed as inadequate — these are precisely the moments when human beings, stripped of the familiar scaffolding of inherited meaning, have been forced into the terrifying and generative encounter with the fundamental questions of existence that comfortable times allow us to defer indefinitely.

The Italian Renaissance of the fourteenth through seventeenth centuries is the most celebrated instance of this pattern, and it is worth examining in some detail, because the structural parallels with the current moment are both striking and instructive. The Renaissance did not emerge from a society that was flourishing. It emerged from the ashes of a civilization that had been comprehensively shattered. The Black Death of 1347 to 1351 killed between one-third and one-half of Europe's population in the space of four years — a demographic catastrophe without parallel in recorded Western history. It did not merely kill people. It killed the cosmological framework within which those people had understood their lives: the hierarchical, divinely ordered medieval world in which every person had their place, every suffering had its meaning, and the Church had reliable answers to every existential question.

When one-third of a civilization's population dies in four years, the answers stop being reliable. The priest who performed last rites died of the same disease as his parishioners. The prayers that were supposed to intercede with God produced no observable divine response. The social hierarchies that were supposed to reflect divine order dissolved in the chaos of mass death, as serfs fled their manors and merchants climbed over the bodies of fallen aristocrats. The framework that had organized European consciousness for a millennium was, in the most literal sense, on trial. And it was found, in the court of lived experience, to be insufficient.

What emerged from that insufficiency, over the following century and a half, was the Renaissance: a fundamental reimagining of what it meant to be a human being, what the world was for, and what kind of life was worth living within it. It was not a comfortable reimagining. It was contested, anguished, often violent, and conducted in the shadow of continuing plague, political upheaval, and religious conflict. But it produced, in the domain of art, philosophy, science, and political thought, achievements of a richness and originality that no previous era of European civilization had approached.

The pattern is consistent across multiple historical instances. The Axial Age of the sixth and fifth centuries BCE — the period that produced Confucius, the Buddha, Socrates, and the Hebrew prophets, in a remarkable simultaneous flowering across four civilizations — emerged from a context of widespread social disruption, political instability, and the collapse of earlier Bronze Age certainties. The Enlightenment of the seventeenth and eighteenth centuries emerged from the wreckage of the Wars of Religion, which had shattered the assumption that theological consensus could organize European political life. The American and French Revolutions emerged from the contradictions of Enlightenment thought encountering the realities of colonial exploitation and aristocratic privilege.

In each case, the pattern is the same: crisis dissolves the inherited framework, the dissolution creates a terrifying but genuine openness, and within that openness — if the human beings inhabiting it choose engagement over denial, creation over nostalgia, and genuine reckoning over the comfortable repetition of invalidated answers — something genuinely new becomes possible.

We are in such a moment now. The Identity Crash is not merely a disruption of the labor market. It is a civilizational crisis of meaning — a wholesale assault on the framework within which most contemporary human beings have organized their understanding of their own worth, their purpose, and their place in the world. And the Human Renaissance is the name for what becomes possible when that assault is met not with denial or despair, but with the courage to ask, genuinely and without predetermined answers, what a human life is for.

II. What the Renaissance Is Not

Before describing what the Human Renaissance is, it is worth being precise about what it is not — because several of the most tempting misunderstandings of the concept are both common and genuinely dangerous.

The Human Renaissance is not a return to the past. It does not involve the abandonment of artificial intelligence, the rejection of technological progress, or the romantic retreatism of those who imagine that the solution to the disruptions of modernity is a return to pre-modern forms of life. The Luddite impulse — the impulse to destroy the machines rather than reimagine the human relationship to them — is understandable as an expression of genuine suffering, but it is not a viable response to a transition that is already underway and cannot be reversed. The machine is not going away. The question is not whether to live with it but how.

The Human Renaissance is not a consolation prize for the cognitively displaced. It is not the argument that since AI can now do the important things, human beings should content themselves with the less important ones — the warm, fuzzy, interpersonal dimensions of life that the machines have not yet got around to commoditizing. This framing is both condescending and false. The capabilities and forms of value that the Human Renaissance centers — embodied intelligence, genuine moral reasoning, creative disruption, authentic empathy, the wisdom that emerges from lived experience — are not lesser capabilities than the cognitive processing that AI is displacing. They are, in many respects, more fundamental, more distinctively human, and more consequential for the quality of human life and the health of human civilization than the information-processing activities that the knowledge economy spent two centuries elevating to the status of primary human value.

The Human Renaissance is not an individual project of personal optimization. It is not a self-help program, a productivity hack, or a rebranding of human capabilities in terms that will generate a new kind of market value. The temptation to respond to the Identity Crash by identifying the specific human capabilities that AI cannot yet replicate and marketing them aggressively — "the five human skills that will still be valuable in 2030" — is real, and the genre of content it produces is voluminous. But it reproduces, rather than challenges, the fundamental error of the Church of the Grind: the assumption that human value must be defined in terms of market utility, and that the appropriate response to the erosion of one form of market utility is the rapid development of another.

The Human Renaissance is, instead, a civilizational reorientation: a fundamental shift in the organizing principle of human value away from productive utility and toward what might be called, with full awareness of the term's philosophical weight, genuine flourishing. Not the flourishing of the market, but the flourishing of persons: the conditions under which human beings are able to live fully, relate genuinely, create authentically, and engage with the irreducible complexity and beauty of existence in ways that the Church of the Grind systematically prevented and the post-Efficiency Wall world is, for the first time in centuries, actively making possible.

III. The Body Reclaimed: Embodiment as Knowledge

The first domain of the Human Renaissance is the one that is, in some respects, most immediately accessible and most immediately healing: the recovery of the body as a primary site of human knowledge, value, and identity.

Artificial intelligence systems are, at their most fundamental level, disembodied. They exist as patterns of mathematical weights in silicon, processing information about the world without any direct sensory relationship to it. They can describe the smell of rain on hot pavement with extraordinary precision — drawing on millions of human descriptions of that smell from the textual record of human experience. But they have never smelled rain on hot pavement. They cannot. The experience is not available to them. And the knowledge that resides in that experience — the specific, irreducible, somatic knowledge of what it is like to be a body in a world of sensory richness — is knowledge that they categorically lack.

This distinction between knowing about something and knowing it through direct embodied experience is one of the oldest and most important in the philosophical tradition. Aristotle's concept of phronesis — practical wisdom — was grounded in the recognition that certain forms of knowing cannot be reduced to propositional knowledge and cannot be acquired through instruction. They require experience: the specific kind of knowledge that accrues through sustained, embodied engagement with the domain in question. The master craftsman does not merely know more propositions about woodworking than the apprentice. They inhabit a different relationship to wood: a sensorimotor intelligence, built through years of physical engagement, that allows them to know in their hands what the apprentice can only know in their head.

The Church of the Grind, in its emphasis on cognitive labor and informational productivity, systematically devalued this kind of embodied knowledge. The knowledge worker's hands were incidental to their professional value. What mattered was what happened between their ears: the logical processing, the pattern recognition, the strategic reasoning that could be expressed in the professional outputs that the market rewarded. The body was a vehicle for transporting the brain to the office, a biological support system for the cognitive apparatus that constituted the person's real economic contribution.

The Human Renaissance inverts this hierarchy. It recognizes, based on both philosophical tradition and contemporary neuroscience, that the body is not a vehicle for the brain but an integral component of the knowing system that we call a person. The research on embodied cognition — the study of how thought is shaped by the specific physical properties of the body that thinks it — has accumulated, over the past three decades, a body of evidence that is both scientifically compelling and philosophically profound. We think with our bodies. Our spatial reasoning is grounded in our experience of navigating three-dimensional space. Our temporal reasoning is grounded in the rhythms of our biological processes. Our emotional reasoning is grounded in the visceral, somatic signals of our autonomic nervous system. Cognition is not a disembodied computation that happens to occur in a biological housing. It is a biological process through and through, and its specifically human character is inseparable from its specifically human embodiment.

The practical implications of this for the Human Renaissance are significant. The recovery of embodied knowledge begins with the recovery of physical craft: the making of things with one's hands, in engagement with the resistance and responsiveness of physical materials. Not as a nostalgic exercise or a hobby in the diminished sense of a leisure activity that one undertakes in the time left over from real life. But as a genuine form of knowing: a way of being in the world that develops capabilities, builds character, and produces a kind of satisfaction that no amount of cognitive processing can replicate.

The woodworker who has spent years learning to read the grain of wood — to feel with their hands where the material wants to go and where it will resist, to understand through repeated physical engagement the specific intelligence of a specific medium — possesses a form of knowledge that is irreplaceable, untransferable, and immune to automation. Not because wood is difficult for robots to process, though in many respects it is. But because the knowledge that the woodworker has developed is not stored in the wood or in any external representation of the relationship between tool and material. It is stored in the nervous system of the woodworker themselves: in the neural pathways that connect intention to movement to sensation to adjustment, built through years of embodied practice and resident nowhere else.

This principle extends beyond craft into the full range of embodied human activity: athletics, cooking, music, dance, surgery, gardening, building, healing through touch. In each of these domains, the Human Renaissance calls for a recovery of the specific form of knowing that resides in sustained, skilled, physically engaged activity — not as a compensation for lost cognitive value, but as a recognition that this form of knowing was always more fundamentally human, and more genuinely irreplaceable, than the cognitive processing that the knowledge economy mistook for the primary product of a human life.

IV. The Gardener and the Algorithm: On Manual Work as Ontological Resistance

There is a particular kind of morning that the Human Renaissance makes available, and that the Church of the Grind never could. It begins not with the opening of a laptop or the checking of a phone, but with the pulling of weeds from a garden bed, or the shaping of clay on a wheel, or the planing of a piece of wood, or the kneading of bread dough, or the tending of a beehive. It is a morning in which the first hour of consciousness is spent in direct, physical, sensory engagement with the material world — in a relationship with a nonhuman reality that has its own requirements, its own resistances, and its own forms of beauty that cannot be optimized, accelerated, or improved by any algorithm.

The garden does not care about your productivity metrics. The clay does not respond to your performance review. The bread dough does not know your job title or your LinkedIn follower count. These materials make their demands — the garden requires watering in heat and drainage in flood; the clay requires attention to moisture and pressure; the dough requires the specific quality of tactile judgment that recognizes the moment of perfect development by feel rather than by timer — and those demands are organized entirely around the logic of the material itself, not around the logic of the market.

This is what makes engagement with manual craft an act of what might be called ontological resistance: a practice that, by its very structure, insists on a relationship with reality that is not mediated by the attention economy, not optimized for market outcomes, and not reducible to the informational categories that AI systems process. The gardener who spends an hour pulling weeds is not merely doing a task. They are inhabiting a mode of being — a specific quality of sensory presence, physical engagement, and direct relationship with the natural world — that is precisely what the digital attention economy is designed to prevent and precisely what the Human Renaissance needs to recover.

The philosophical tradition has something important to say about the value of this kind of engagement. Matthew Crawford's 2009 book Shop Class as Soulcraft made the case, with both philosophical rigor and personal testimony, that manual work is not a lesser form of human activity than intellectual work, but a different and in some respects richer one: a form of engagement with the world that demands genuine attention, genuine skill, and genuine respect for the independent reality of the materials and tools with which one works. Crawford's craftsman — the motorcycle mechanic, the pipe organ restorer, the millwright — inhabits a world of genuine complexity and genuine feedback, a world in which errors have visible consequences and excellence has palpable results, a world that is, in this specific sense, more fully real than the world of the knowledge worker whose outputs are always mediated by layers of abstraction.

In the context of the Identity Crash, the value of manual work is not merely philosophical. It is psychological and neurological. The specific quality of attention that skilled manual work requires — the sustained, present-moment focus on the specific demands of a specific material in a specific condition, without the possibility of distraction or multitasking that cognitive work permits — is precisely the quality of attention that the Dopamine Trap is most systematically eroding. The person who maintains a daily practice of skilled manual engagement is not merely keeping an interesting hobby. They are maintaining and developing the attentional capacity that the digital environment is working, with considerable sophistication, to destroy.

V. IRRATIONALITY REVISITED: THE INTELLIGENCE OF THE WRONG TURN

The second domain of the Human Renaissance is the most philosophically interesting and the most genuinely difficult to describe in terms that do justice to its full significance: the human capacity for productive irrationality. For the kind of thinking that follows intuition against evidence, that trusts a perception that the data does not support, that makes the wrong turn and finds, on the other side of it, something that the right turn could never have reached.

This capacity is systematically undervalued in the culture of the Church of the Grind, which prizes above all the rational, evidence-based, outcome-optimizing forms of cognition that can be documented in a performance review and justified to a committee. It is systematically absent from AI systems, which are, by architecture and training, anchored to the patterns of their data and incapable of genuine departure from them. And it is systematically essential to every form of human creative and intellectual achievement that has genuinely advanced the boundaries of what is known and what is possible.

The neuroscientific basis of productive irrationality is increasingly well understood. The human brain operates in two broad modes that the psychologist Daniel Kahneman famously described as System 1 and System 2: the fast, intuitive, associative, emotionally inflected mode of cognition that operates beneath conscious awareness, and the slow, deliberate, logical, consciously controlled mode that constitutes what we typically mean by "reasoning." Both systems are genuine forms of intelligence. Both contribute to effective cognition and good decision-making. The error of the Church of the Grind — and of the optimization culture it produced — is the assumption that System 2 reasoning is the higher and more reliable form of the two, and that System 1 intuition is merely a source of bias to be corrected.

The research does not support this assumption. In domains of genuine complexity — domains where the relevant variables are too numerous to be held in conscious awareness simultaneously, where the relationships between variables are nonlinear and context-dependent, and where the most valuable information is not quantifiable or articulable — System 1 intuition frequently outperforms System 2 reasoning. The expert clinician who trusts a "gut feeling" that something is wrong with a patient, despite normal test results, is not being irrational. They are drawing on a reservoir of pattern recognition built from thousands of clinical encounters, processed at a level of neural integration that conscious reasoning cannot access and that produces outputs — the felt sense that something requires attention — that are frequently more accurate than the outputs of explicit analytical reasoning applied to the same data.

This is the intelligence of the wrong turn. Not the wrong turn of ignorance or carelessness, but the wrong turn of the person who has developed enough genuine expertise to trust the perceptions that their explicit reasoning cannot yet account for. The artist who abandons the technically correct composition in favor of the one that feels right. The entrepreneur who pursues the opportunity that the market research says is too small to be worthwhile, because they have a perception of an unmet need that the research methodology is too blunt to capture. The scientist who takes seriously an anomalous result that every statistical convention says should be dismissed as noise, because something in their accumulated experience tells them the anomaly is real.

AI systems cannot make these wrong turns because they are, by construction, systems of pattern completion: they navigate toward the most probable outcome given the patterns of their training data. They can generate novelty within established patterns. They cannot genuinely depart from those patterns. The human capacity to trust a perception that the data does not yet support — to be willing to be wrong in public, to follow an intuition into territory where the evidence is thin and the risk of failure is high — is not a residual irrationality to be trained out of the next generation of professionals. It is one of the most precious capacities that human beings bring to the world.

Cultivating this capacity in the context of the Human Renaissance means, among other things, creating the conditions under which it can operate: the tolerance for uncertainty, the willingness to be confused for longer than comfort requires, the practice of attending to one's own perceptions and intuitions rather than immediately subjecting them to the rationalizing pressure of "what does the data say?" It means developing what the philosopher Michael Polanyi called "tacit knowledge" — the knowledge that we know more than we can tell — and learning to trust that knowledge rather than dismissing it in the absence of explicit justification.

VI. The Creative Act as Human Signature

Closely related to productive irrationality but deserving its own examination is the specific human capacity for genuine creative disruption: the ability to produce work that does not merely extend or recombine existing patterns but fundamentally challenges, transforms, or transcends them. This is the capacity that distinguishes the artist from the craftsman, the revolutionary scientist from the diligent experimenter, the genuine innovator from the skilled improver. And it is, of all the human capacities discussed in this chapter, the one most frequently claimed as the last redoubt of human uniqueness in the face of advancing AI — and the one whose claimed invulnerability requires the most careful and honest examination.

AI systems can produce creative work. This is not in dispute. Large language models can write poetry that is technically accomplished and occasionally moving. Generative image models can produce visual art that is aesthetically sophisticated and genuinely beautiful. Music generation systems can compose in a wide range of styles with remarkable fidelity to the conventions of those styles. Anyone who denies the creative capabilities of current AI systems is not engaging honestly with the evidence.

But there is a distinction — philosophically important and significant — between the creativity of pattern recombination and the creativity of genuine disruption. AI creative work, however, technically sophisticated, is fundamentally the creativity of the former kind: it recombines, extrapolates, and synthesizes within the patterns of its training data with extraordinary skill. What it cannot do is genuinely transcend those patterns — cannot produce work that challenges the aesthetic, intellectual, or moral frameworks within which it was trained, because it has no relationship to those frameworks other than as patterns in data. It cannot be disturbed by its own work, cannot find itself saying something it did not intend to say, cannot be led by the work itself into territory that surprises and unsettles the maker.

The human creative act, at its most genuine, has exactly this quality. The painter who begins with an intention and finds, in the act of painting, that the work is telling them something they did not know. The novelist whose characters develop, while writing, into people the author did not plan and cannot fully control. The composer who discovers, in the working out of a harmonic problem, a resolution that changes their understanding of what harmony can do. These are not descriptions of technical process. They are descriptions of a genuine encounter between a conscious maker and the medium of their making — an encounter in which the maker is changed by what they make, in ways that no algorithm can experience because algorithms are not changed by their outputs.

The Human Renaissance calls for a recovery of this relationship to creative work: not creative work as content production, not creative work as personal branding, or market positioning, but creative work as a genuine practice of self-knowledge and self-transformation. The person who writes not to publish but to understand what they think. The person who paints not to produce saleable images but to develop their capacity to see. The person who makes music not to accumulate streaming plays but to inhabit the specific quality of temporal experience that music makes possible. These are not hobbies in the diminished sense of idle pastimes. They are practices of becoming — ways of developing, through sustained creative engagement, the specific dimensions of selfhood that the Church of the Grind suppressed and the Human Renaissance needs to recover.

VII. Shared Suffering: The Irreplaceable Foundation of Genuine Care

The third and in many ways most foundational domain of the Human Renaissance is the capacity for genuine empathy — for the specific form of understanding and care that emerges from the shared condition of human vulnerability, finitude, and suffering. This is not a peripheral or optional component of the Human Renaissance. It is its ethical and relational core: the ground from which everything else grows.

The word "empathy" has been used in so many ways, and with so much sentimental imprecision, that it has become difficult to use with the rigor that the concept deserves. For the purposes of this chapter, empathy means something specific: the capacity to genuinely understand another person's experience from the inside — not merely to recognize that they are suffering, not merely to have access to information about the nature of their suffering, but to have a lived sense of what it is like to be them in the situation they are inhabiting. And this capacity, in its genuine form, is grounded in something that artificial systems categorically lack: the experience of suffering.

A machine can know that you are suffering. It can have access to every documented account of human suffering ever written, every clinical description of every form of pain, every first-person narrative of grief, loss, fear, and despair that has been committed to text. It can process this information with extraordinary accuracy and produce responses that are calibrated with great sophistication to the specific nature and context of your suffering. These responses can be genuinely helpful. In a world of widespread human loneliness and inadequate access to human care, even a sophisticated simulation of empathy has real value.

But it is not genuine empathy. Genuine empathy is not a response calibrated to the description of suffering. It is a resonance between two nervous systems that have both experienced suffering — a recognition that is grounded not in information but in shared ontological condition. When a therapist who has navigated their own episode of severe depression sits with a client who is in the grip of one, what passes between them is not merely information and technique. It is the specific quality of recognition that can only come from one who has been there: the knowledge, carried in the body and expressed in the quality of attention, that this person is not alone in the universe because there is someone in the room who has been in this same darkness and found their way toward the light.

This form of recognition — what the philosopher Simone Weil called "the creative attention that constitutes love" — is not a minor or marginal human capacity. It is the foundation of every form of genuine human care: medicine, therapy, teaching, friendship, parenting, spiritual guidance, political leadership at its best. It is the capacity that makes it possible for one human being to genuinely help another through the specific forms of suffering that only a human life entails: the grief of bereavement, the terror of serious illness, the shame of failure, the loneliness of the misunderstood, the despair of the meaningless existence.

The Human Renaissance calls for a recovery of the willingness to be genuinely present to each other in these dimensions of experience: not as efficient care providers, not as information processors or resource connectors, but as fellow sufferers and fellow survivors. This requires a quality of availability and openness that the Church of the Grind systematically discouraged — the willingness to be moved, to be affected, to allow another person's reality to penetrate the professional armor of competent functionality and reach the human being who lives beneath it.

It requires the willingness to acknowledge one's own vulnerability: to be seen as someone who has suffered, who has been afraid, who has failed, who has been lost. This acknowledgment is not weakness. In the context of the Human Renaissance, it is the primary credential of genuine care — the evidence that the care being offered is grounded in real human experience rather than performed from a position of untouchable competence.

VIII. The Community of Presence: Beyond the Network

The Human Renaissance is not solely an individual project. It cannot be accomplished alone, and any version of it that attempts to locate the full weight of human flourishing in the interior life of the individual self is misunderstanding both the nature of human beings and the specific character of what the Identity Crash has taken away.

The Church of the Grind, in its emphasis on individual productivity and professional achievement, produced a specific and recognizable social pathology: the professional who has an extraordinary network and no genuine community. Thousands of contacts on LinkedIn. Hundreds of colleagues and clients and professional acquaintances. And, in the quiet hours, the specific kind of loneliness that comes from being known extensively but not deeply — from having a social existence organized entirely around professional utility, in which the relationships that constitute one's social world exist primarily as means to professional ends rather than as ends in themselves.

The research on social connection and human wellbeing is unambiguous on this point: what produces genuine psychological health, genuine resilience, and genuine life satisfaction is not the breadth of social network but the depth of genuine community. The Harvard Study of Adult Development, the longest-running study of adult health and happiness in history, has tracked its participants for over eighty years and arrived at a finding of deceptive simplicity: the single most reliable predictor of health, happiness, and longevity is the quality of close personal relationships. Not wealth. Not professional achievement. Not even physical health, though that matters. Relationships: the specific experience of being genuinely known by, and genuinely committed to, a small number of other human beings over time.

Genuine community — the kind that produces this quality of mutual knowledge and mutual commitment — cannot be constructed through network-building strategies or professional relationship management. It requires what the sociologist Robert Nisbet called "the quest for community": the sustained, often inconvenient, frequently challenging work of maintaining the face-to-face, time-intensive, mutually demanding relationships within which people genuinely come to know each other, genuinely come to care about each other, and genuinely become part of each other's lives in ways that persist through difficulty and change.

The Human Renaissance, in this domain, involves a recovery of the willingness to invest in community as a primary value rather than as a pleasant supplement to professional life. The neighborhood association, the reading group, the religious community, the sports club, the mutual aid network, the informal gathering of friends who meet regularly and know each other's lives — these are not peripheral to the Human Renaissance. They are its social infrastructure: the webs of genuine relationship within which the specific human capacities of shared suffering, genuine care, embodied presence, and creative community become possible.

Building and maintaining these webs requires exactly the qualities that the post-Efficiency Wall world is making available and the Dopamine Trap is working to prevent: the willingness to be present, to be slow, to be inconvenient, to invest time and attention in relationships that will not generate any immediately measurable return. The neighbor who shows up with food when someone is ill. The friend who sits through the long, rambling conversation that doesn't arrive at any conclusion but matters because it was had. The community member who attends the meeting, does the unglamorous organizational work, and maintains the institutions that make collective life possible. These are acts of the Human Renaissance. They are, in their quiet and unheroic way, the most important acts of resistance available to a person navigating the Identity Crash.

IX. The New Humanism: A Value System for the Post-Utility Age

The Human Renaissance requires a new humanism: a coherent and philosophically grounded value system that can organize a life in the post-utility age with the same clarity and force that the work ethic organized a life in the industrial age. Not a set of platitudes or motivational aphorisms, but a genuine intellectual framework — one that can answer the fundamental questions of value and purpose that the Identity Crash has placed back on the table.

The new humanism begins with a single foundational claim: that the value of a human life is not a function of its productive output. That human beings are valuable not because of what they produce but because of what they are: conscious, embodied, relational, temporally situated creatures who experience the world from a specific and irreplaceable perspective, who suffer and love and create and care in ways that have intrinsic significance regardless of any market assessment of their economic contribution.

This claim is not new. It is, in various formulations, the foundational claim of every major humanist tradition in Western and non-Western philosophy. Kant's insistence that persons are ends in themselves, never merely means. The Buddhist teaching on the inherent dignity of all sentient beings. The Christian doctrine of the imago Dei: that every human being carries within them the image of the divine, a dignity that precedes and transcends any social role or productive function. The Confucian emphasis on the cultivation of human relationships as the primary moral task of a life. These traditions differ enormously in their metaphysical foundations and their practical prescriptions. They converge, with remarkable consistency, on the rejection of the claim that human worth is reducible to productive utility.

What is new, in the current moment, is the historical pressure that is forcing this ancient claim from the domain of philosophical aspiration into the domain of practical necessity. For two centuries, the work ethic provided a functional — if philosophically confused and psychologically costly — answer to the question of human worth. It was wrong, but it worked, in the specific sense that it provided a stable basis for individual identity and social organization in the conditions of industrial capitalism. The Identity Crash has destroyed the conditions under which that answer worked. The new humanism is not being advocated merely as a philosophical improvement on the work ethic. It is being proposed as the only adequate response to a situation in which the work ethic's answer has been rendered not merely philosophically unsatisfying but insufficient.

The practical content of the new humanism is organized around three principles that correspond to the three domains of human irreplaceability described in this chapter. The first is the principle of embodied engagement: the commitment to maintaining and developing one's capacities for skilled, sensory, physically present engagement with the material world and with other human bodies. The second is the principle of creative authenticity: the commitment to genuine creative practice as a form of self-knowledge and self-development, conducted for its own sake rather than for market validation. The third is the principle of relational depth: the commitment to the sustained, demanding, and irreplaceable work of genuine community and genuine care.

These principles are not a program. They do not specify the form that embodied engagement, creative authenticity, or relational depth should take for any specific person. They are a direction: the direction away from the Church of the Grind's definition of a well-lived life and toward something that the human beings who have always known better — the artists, the craftspeople, the healers, the teachers, the contemplatives — have been demonstrating, in the margins of the knowledge economy, for as long as the knowledge economy has existed.

X. The Second Genesis: What Becomes Possible

Every genuine renaissance produces things that were not predictable from the conditions that preceded it. The Italian Renaissance produced Michelangelo's Sistine Chapel, Leonardo's notebooks, Machiavelli's political philosophy, Brunelleschi's dome. None of these were legible as possibilities from within the framework of medieval European culture that the Renaissance displaced. They emerged from the specific collision of old and new, the specific combination of inherited resources and radical openness, that the crisis and its aftermath made available.

The Human Renaissance will produce its own things that are not yet predictable. New forms of art that emerge from the specific collision of human embodied intelligence and AI-generated pattern. New forms of community that develop in response to the specific social conditions of the post-Efficiency Wall world. New philosophical frameworks for thinking about consciousness, identity, and value that the encounter with genuinely capable AI is forcing into existence. New forms of craft, healing, education, and political organization that the redistribution of cognitive labor is making possible and necessary.

What can be said, with some confidence, is the direction of these developments. They will be characterized by a renewed emphasis on presence over representation: on the experience of being genuinely in a place, with genuinely specific other people, engaging with genuinely particular materials and concerns, rather than the mediated, abstracted, always-available-everywhere experience that the digital environment provides and that the Human Renaissance must complement rather than replicate. They will be characterized by a renewed emphasis on depth over breadth: on the intensive cultivation of specific capabilities, specific relationships, and specific communities rather than the perpetual expansion of the professional network, the personal brand, and the portfolio of marketable skills.

And they will be characterized, above all, by a renewed emphasis on being over doing: on the quality of engagement with experience rather than the quantity of outputs generated, on the richness of the inner life rather than the impressiveness of the professional résumé, on the depth of one's relationship with the people and places and practices that constitute one's actual life rather than with the abstract career trajectory that the Church of the Grind mistook for the point.

This is the Second Genesis that the Identity Crash makes available. Not a return to an imagined pre-lapsarian innocence, not a retreat into nostalgic comfort, but an advance — difficult, demanding, and potentially extraordinary — into a form of human life that has never quite existed before: one that is post-scarcity in the material sense, post-labor in the cognitive sense, and therefore, for the first time in the long history of human civilization, free to ask the question that every wisdom tradition has always said was the most important one.

Not what I am worth to the market. But what does it mean to live well.

The Renaissance is not behind us. It is what we choose to make of what has been unmade.

CHAPTER SEVEN

THE POST-UTILITY BLUEPRINT

✦ ✦ ✦

I. THE GAP BETWEEN VISION AND ARCHITECTURE

Every meaningful transformation in human life follows the same two-stage structure. The first stage is conceptual: the shift in understanding that makes a new way of living thinkable, that dissolves the old framework and creates the intellectual space in which something genuinely different becomes imaginable. The second stage is architectural: the translation of that new understanding into the specific, concrete, daily structures, and practices through which a life is lived. The first stage without the second produces insight without change. The second without the first produces discipline without direction. Both are necessary, and neither is sufficient alone.

The preceding chapters of this book have been primarily concerned with the first stage: the dissolution of the Church of the Grind's framework, the diagnosis of the specific pathologies of the transition, and the articulation of the Human Renaissance as a vision of what becomes possible on the other side of the Identity Crash. If those chapters have done their work, the reader arrives at this one with a changed understanding: a genuine sense of what has been lost and why its loss is, in some essential respect, a liberation; a clear picture of the traps that await the person who navigates the transition without awareness; and a meaningful sense of the specific human capacities and forms of value that the post-Efficiency Wall world is revealing as genuinely, irreducibly important.

But understanding is not enough. The person who has genuinely absorbed the preceding chapters and then returns to a daily life whose structure is unchanged has acquired a more sophisticated account of their own dissatisfaction without acquiring the tools to address it. The vision of the Human Renaissance, without an architecture for living it, remains an aspiration — and aspirations, in the face of the Dopamine Trap, the organizational pressures of ghost employment, and the deep habits of mind cultivated by decades of Church of the Grind conditioning, are fragile things.

This chapter is the architecture. It is the specific, practical, and deliberately honest account of what it takes to build a daily life organized around the values of the Human Renaissance rather than the values of the Church of the Grind. Not a program to be followed with rigid precision, but a blueprint — a set of structural principles and specific practices that, taken together, create the conditions under which a genuinely different kind of life becomes not merely imaginable but habitable.

The blueprint rests on three foundational practices. They are not the only practices that matter in the post-utility life, but they are the ones that create the conditions under which every other valuable practice becomes possible. They are the load-bearing walls of the new architecture. Without them, the structure collapses back into the familiar patterns of the old one, regardless of how sincere the aspiration to build something different might be.

The three practices are the Deep Hour, the Physical Anchor, and the Micro-Economy of Meaning. Each will be examined in depth in the sections that follow, with attention not merely to what the practice involves but to why it works, what it produces over time, and what the specific challenges of implementation look like in the actual conditions of a real life in the current moment.

II. The Neuroscience of Daily Structure

Before examining each of the three practices individually, it is worth establishing the neurological and psychological foundation that makes the entire blueprint coherent: the understanding of why daily structure matters so much more than most people realize, and why the specific timing, sequence, and quality of the first hours of each day have an influence on the entire day's psychological character that is disproportionate to the fraction of the day they represent.

The human brain does not begin each day in a neutral state. It begins in a state that has been shaped, in complex and partially predictable ways, by the previous day's experiences, the quality of the preceding night's sleep, the hormonal fluctuations of the morning cortisol awakening response, and the specific neural patterns that have been reinforced by months and years of habitual behavior in the first hours of each morning. The brain that has spent three years beginning every day by immediately reaching for the phone and checking notifications has trained its attentional and reward systems to orient, first thing in the morning, toward the externally directed, algorithmically stimulated engagement that the phone provides. This training is not merely a habit in the colloquial sense of a practice that can be changed by a sufficiently firm resolution. It is a genuine neurological condition: a set of established neural pathways that have been reinforced through repeated activation to the point where they represent the path of least resistance for the morning brain.

Conversely, the brain that has spent three years beginning every day with an hour of analog engagement — reading, writing, physical craft, or quiet reflection — has trained its attentional and reward systems to orient, first thing in the morning, toward the internally directed, self-paced, genuinely engaging forms of activity that constitute the Deep Hour. This is not merely a matter of willpower. It is a neurological reality: the morning brain, conditioned through sustained practice, arrives at the beginning of the day already primed for the kind of engagement that sustains, rather than erodes, genuine human capacities.

The practical implication is both simple and demanding: the most important behavioral change available to the person building a post-utility life is the change that happens first thing in the morning, before the day's competing demands have assembled and before the attentional habits of the previous day have had a chance to reassert themselves. The morning is the leverage point. What happens in the first hour establishes the psychological tone, the attentional orientation, and the behavioral momentum that will shape everything that follows. Getting the morning right is not the whole of the post-utility blueprint. But it is the part that makes the rest of it possible.

The morning cortisol awakening response — the sharp spike in cortisol that occurs in the first thirty to forty-five minutes after waking, and that functions as a biological alerting signal preparing the organism for the demands of the day ahead — is a window of particular importance for establishing the day's cognitive and attentional character. Research on the relationship between the cortisol awakening response and subsequent cognitive performance suggests that the activities engaged in during this window have an influence on subsequent cognitive functioning that is disproportionate to their duration. The person who spends this window in deep analog engagement — in reading, writing, creative work, or physical practice that demands genuine attentional investment — is, in a neurological sense, setting the terms for the day's cognitive functioning in a way that later-day interventions cannot fully replicate.

III. The Deep Hour: Anatomy of an Ancient Practice

The Deep Hour is not a new idea dressed in contemporary language. It is the contemporary formulation of a practice that appears, in various forms, in every wisdom tradition and in the personal routines of a remarkable proportion of the most creatively productive human beings in history. The specific form it takes varies enormously: the deep hour of Montaigne was the morning spent in his tower library, reading and writing in the essays that would become one of the foundational texts of Western humanistic self-examination. The deep hour of Darwin was the morning walk along the "thinking path" he constructed at Down House, during which the observations and associations of the previous day were allowed to incubate and combine. The deep hour of Toni Morrison was the pre-dawn writing session that she maintained through the years of raising children and working full-time, the only window of uninterrupted consciousness available to her.

What these varied practices share is the common structure that defines the Deep Hour: a period of sustained, self-directed, analog engagement at the beginning of the day, before the external world has made its demands, before the digital environment has captured the attentional system, and before the cognitive resources of the morning have been spent on activities that serve other people's agendas rather than the development of one's own inner life.

The word "analog" in the definition of the Deep Hour is not incidental. It is a specific and important requirement. The distinction between analog and digital engagement is not merely a distinction between old and innovative technologies. It is a distinction between two fundamentally different relationships between the human mind and the objects of its attention. Digital engagement — even digital engagement with genuinely valuable content, such as reading a book on an e-reader or writing in a digital journal — occurs in an environment of perpetual potential interruption: the notification that might arrive, the temptation to check another tab, the subtle but persistent awareness of connectivity that the digital device maintains even when its most disruptive features are temporarily disabled. The analog engagement of a physical book, a handwritten journal, a wooden surface being shaped by a hand tool, or a musical instrument being played, occurs in an environment of genuine discontinuity from the digital world: a space of pure attention to the object immediately present, undiluted by the awareness of what might be happening elsewhere.

This distinction matters neurologically. The research on attention and the effects of digital connectivity on sustained focus is consistent: the mere presence of a smartphone on a desk, even face-down and silenced, measurably reduces the cognitive resources available for the task at hand, because a portion of attentional capacity is continuously devoted to the monitoring and suppression of the impulse to check it. Genuine analog engagement — engagement that occurs in physical environments where the digital option is genuinely absent rather than merely suppressed —

allows the full mobilization of attentional resources in a way that digitally adjacent activities cannot.

The specific content of the Deep Hour matters less than its structural properties: that it is analog, that it is self-directed rather than externally assigned, that it engages genuine cognitive or creative capacity rather than merely occupying time, and that it is conducted with sufficient regularity to produce the neurological conditioning described in the previous section. Within these structural requirements, the range of possible Deep Hour practices is as diverse as the range of human interests and capacities.

For many people, the most powerful form of the Deep Hour is reading — specifically, reading long-form, demanding texts that require the kind of sustained, patient attention that the digital environment has made progressively harder to maintain. Not the reading of news articles or social media posts, which is structured around the same variable-ratio reward logic as other digital engagement, but the reading of books: texts that develop a sustained argument or narrative over hundreds of pages, that require the reader to hold a complex structure in working memory over days and weeks of engagement, and that reward patience with the specific pleasure of deep understanding that shallow reading cannot produce.

For others, the Deep Hour takes the form of writing — not the writing of emails or reports or professional communications, but the writing of a private journal, a notebook of observations and reflections, a practice of putting one's own experience into words without any audience other than oneself. The research on the psychological benefits of expressive writing — developed primarily through the work of James Pennebaker at the University of Texas — is substantial and consistent: the regular practice of writing about one's own experiences, thoughts, and feelings produces measurable improvements in psychological wellbeing, immune function, and the capacity for cognitive integration of difficult experiences. These benefits are not produced by the quality of the writing, by its literary merit, or by any external validation of its content. They are produced by the practice itself: by the specific cognitive process of translating lived experience into language, with its demands for coherence, specificity, and honest self-observation.

For still others — and this form of the Deep Hour is perhaps the most undervalued and the most important for the specific population most vulnerable to the Identity Crash — the hour takes the form of creative practice: the daily engagement with a medium — drawing, music, woodworking, ceramics, photography, poetry, cooking as art rather than function — that demands genuine skill, responds to genuine attention, and develops, through sustained practice over time, a form of competence and aesthetic sensitivity that is irreducibly the practitioner's own.

IV. The Deep Hour in Practice: Obstacles and Their Navigation

The theoretical case for the Deep Hour is, to most people who encounter it, immediately compelling. The practical implementation is, for most of those same people, significantly harder than the theory suggests. The obstacles are real, and they deserve honest examination rather than the dismissive reassurance that "anyone can find an hour in the morning if they really want to." Some people genuinely cannot, given the specific demands of their current life circumstances. But many people who believe they cannot face a different problem: not the absence of the hour, but the presence of habits, environments, and psychological patterns that make the hour feel unavailable even when it is technically present.

The most common obstacle is the phone. The habit of checking the phone within the first minutes of waking is, for a substantial proportion of the adult population of the developed world, the single most deeply entrenched behavioral pattern of the day — more automatic, more resistant to deliberate change, and more neurologically established than almost any other behavior in the daily repertoire. Breaking this habit does not require willpower. It requires environmental design: the removal of the phone from the bedroom, the establishment of a charging station in another room, the use of a physical alarm clock rather than a phone alarm, and the creation of a morning environment in which the analog alternative is physically present and immediately accessible.

The second common obstacle is the competing claim of genuine responsibilities: the child who wakes early, the partner whose schedule constrains the morning, the job whose early demands cannot be deferred.

For people in these circumstances, the Deep Hour may not be available in the morning. The structural principle — that a daily period of sustained, self-directed analog engagement is essential to the post-utility life — remains valid even if the timing must be adjusted. The early evening, the lunch break, the period immediately after the children are in bed: these can all serve as windows for the Deep Hour if the morning is genuinely unavailable. What cannot be adjusted is the commitment to finding the window and protecting it with the same intentionality that one would bring to any genuinely important appointment.

The third obstacle is the one that is most rarely acknowledged and most psychologically significant: the discomfort of the practice itself, particularly in its initial stages. The person who sits down for the first morning of their Deep Hour with a book or a journal and finds, after ten minutes, that their attention is fragmenting, their mind is pulling toward the phone, and the quiet of the analog space feels less like peace and more like deprivation — this person is not failing at the practice. They are experiencing exactly what the practice is designed to address: the trained restlessness of a nervous system that has been conditioned to expect a level of stimulation that the Deep Hour deliberately withholds.

The correct response to this discomfort is not to push through with white-knuckled determination, which is exhausting and unsustainable, but to treat it with the same patient, interested attention that a meditator brings to the arising of difficult mental states during sitting practice. The discomfort is information. It is the felt experience of a specific neurological condition — the withdrawal from habitual stimulation — and like all forms of withdrawal, it diminishes with time and consistent practice. Most people who maintain the Deep Hour through the first two to three weeks of discomfort report a genuine qualitative shift: a discovery that the quiet of the analog space is not deprivation but richness, that the absence of external stimulation is not emptiness but the precondition for the specific quality of internal engagement that the Deep Hour is designed to cultivate.

V. The Physical Anchor: The Body as Bastion

The second foundational practice of the post-utility blueprint is the Physical Anchor: a daily commitment to an embodied physical practice that is demanding enough to require genuine presence and sustained enough to develop genuine capacity over time. It is called an anchor because it performs, in the architecture of the post-utility life, the function that a ship's anchor performs in a harbor: it prevents drift. It keeps the person connected to the most fundamental dimension of their existence — the fact of being a body in the physical world — in a period when the forces of the Identity Crash and the Dopamine Trap are systematically working to untether them from that dimension.

The Physical Anchor is not a gym routine, though it can take that form. It is not a fitness program, a weight loss strategy, or a performance optimization protocol, though it may produce benefits in all these domains as secondary effects of a practice organized around an entirely different primary purpose. The Physical Anchor is a daily practice of genuine physical challenge undertaken not primarily for its health benefits — though these are real and well-documented — but for the specific psychological and existential benefits that genuine physical challenge uniquely provides.

The most important of these benefits is the experience of genuine difficulty genuinely met. In an environment increasingly organized around the elimination of friction — where every cognitive challenge can be outsourced to an AI system, where every social interaction can be mediated by a device, and where every uncomfortable emotion can be managed by an algorithmically curated distraction — the experience of choosing difficulty and staying with it through the hard parts is one of the most countercultural and psychologically valuable things a person can do. The Physical Anchor provides this experience in its most basic and most reliable form: the experience of a body being asked to do something hard, resisting, and doing it anyway.

This experience has a specific psychological profile that distinguishes it from other forms of difficulty. Physical challenge is immediate and unambiguous. The weight either moves or it does not. The distance either gets covered or it does not. The wall either gets climbed or it does not. Unlike the diffuse, often invisible challenges of professional life in the post-Efficiency Wall world — where it is often genuinely unclear whether one is contributing something real or merely performing contribution — physical challenge provides clear, unmediated, immediate feedback. The body knows what it has done and what it has not. And the sense of competence — the lived, bodily knowledge of having done something that was genuinely difficult — is one of the most reliable antidotes available to the Uselessness Syndrome that the Identity Crash produces.

The research on the relationship between physical exercise and psychological wellbeing is among the most robust in all of health psychology. Regular vigorous physical activity produces reductions in symptoms of depression and anxiety comparable to those produced by pharmacological interventions, without the side effects and with the additional benefit of developing physical capacity rather than merely managing symptoms. The neurological mechanisms are increasingly well understood: vigorous exercise triggers the release of brain-derived neurotrophic factor (BDNF), a protein that promotes neurogenesis — the growth of new neurons — in the hippocampus, a brain region central to memory, learning, and mood regulation. It produces endorphin-mediated reductions in the subjective experience of pain and anxiety. And it activates the endocannabinoid system in ways that produce genuine and sustained improvements in mood and cognitive function.

But the Physical Anchor is more than a delivery mechanism for neurochemical benefits, however genuine those benefits are. At its deepest level, it is a practice of presence: the daily rediscovery of the body as the site of genuine experience, genuine challenge, and genuine identity. The person who runs three miles every morning does not merely become healthier. They become someone who runs three miles every morning: someone whose identity is partially constituted by the daily encounter with physical challenge, with the specific landscapes and weather conditions of the route, with the gradual development of capacity over weeks and months of consistent practice. This is an identity that no algorithm can automate, no market disruption can devalue, and no organizational restructuring can eliminate. It is rooted in the one substrate that is absolutely, irreversibly, and permanently the person's own: their body.

VI. The Physical Anchor: Forms, Gradations, and the Question of Intricate Skill

The Physical Anchor can take an extraordinary range of forms, and part of the practice of establishing it is the honest self-assessment required to identify the form that will be both genuinely challenging and genuinely sustainable for a specific person in their specific circumstances. The wrong physical practice — one that is too ambitious, too dependent on specific equipment or conditions, or simply misaligned with one's genuine interests and capacities — will not become an anchor. It will become a source of guilt, a failed resolution, and evidence of the kind of inadequacy that the Identity Crash has already produced too much of.

The most sustainable Physical Anchors tend to share several properties. They are accessible: they can be performed without elaborate equipment, special facilities, or significant financial investment. They are scalable: they can be adapted to the person's current physical condition and progressively intensified as capacity develops. They are intrinsically rewarding: they produce, during the practice itself, a quality of experience — effort met, presence achieved, capacity discovered — that motivates continued engagement independently of any external validation or outcome. And they are, in the deepest sense, embodied: they require genuine physical presence and genuine physical effort, and they cannot be performed on autopilot without losing their essential character.

Running, swimming, cycling, rowing, climbing, and the traditional athletic disciplines satisfy these criteria for many people. But the most powerful form of the Physical Anchor, for the purposes of the post-utility blueprint, is one that adds an additional dimension to the straightforward challenge of cardiovascular or strength effort: the dimension of intricate physical skill. The practice that requires not merely physical exertion but the development of specific, fine-grained, embodied competence — the kind of knowing-in-the-hands described in the previous chapter — produces benefits that straightforward effort alone cannot.

Martial arts are the paradigmatic example. The person who commits to a serious martial arts practice — whether Brazilian jiu-jitsu, boxing, wrestling, judo, or any of the traditional Asian martial disciplines — is committing to a practice that demands not merely physical effort but the development of a specific, complex, deeply embodied form of intelligence: the ability to read and respond to another body's movement in real time, with the combination of technical knowledge, physical conditioning, and situational awareness that genuine martial competence requires. This practice develops, over years of consistent training, a form of bodily self-knowledge and self-confidence that is among the most powerful available antidotes to the specific form of identity fragility that the Identity Crash produces.

The same principle applies to rock climbing, which demands a specific form of spatial-physical intelligence in the reading and navigation of vertical terrain. To dance, which demands the integration of musical intelligence, spatial awareness, and expressive physical communication in a way that no amount of cognitive understanding can replace. To the traditional manual crafts — smithing, ceramics, carpentry, masonry — that require the development of specific sensorimotor knowledge through sustained physical engagement with resistant materials. In each case, the Physical Anchor provides not merely the benefits of physical exercise but the additional, specifically irreplaceable benefit of a form of embodied knowing that is genuinely, permanently, and proudly the practitioner's own.

The question of how much time the Physical Anchor requires is one that deserves a direct answer, because it is one of the most common practical obstacles to its implementation. The research on the dose-response relationship between physical activity and psychological benefit suggests that the minimum effective dose — the amount required to produce meaningful, consistent improvements in mood, cognitive function, and psychological resilience — is approximately thirty minutes of moderate to vigorous activity per day, on most days of the week. This is a modest time investment compared to the benefits it produces. The person who cannot find thirty minutes per day for physical practice in a schedule that includes multiple hours per day of digital engagement is not experiencing a genuine time shortage. They are experiencing a prioritization problem that is, at its root, a values problem: a residual commitment to the Church of the Grind's hierarchy of value, which places cognitive and professional activities above physical and embodied ones.

VII. The Micro-Economy of Meaning: A Different Kind of Wealth

The third foundational practice of the post-utility blueprint is the most distinctively human and the most resistant to systematic description: the deliberate construction and maintenance of what this book calls the Micro-Economy of Meaning. It is the most resistant to description because it is the most contextual, the most interpersonal, and the most dependent on the specific circumstances, relationships, and capacities of the individual person. But it is also, in many respects, the most important of the three practices — the one that gives the other two their larger purpose and that prevents the post-utility life from becoming a merely self-cultivating project rather than a genuinely human one.

An economy, in its most general sense, is a system for the production and exchange of value. The Micro-Economy of Meaning is an economy in this sense: a system through which value is produced and exchanged, and through which the participants in the system become richer in the specific currency that the system trades in. But the value it produces and exchanges is not financial. It is the value of genuine human contribution to the lives of specific other human beings: the value of attention freely given, of care genuinely offered, of skill shared without expectation of return, of presence maintained through difficulty, of the specific forms of witness and accompaniment that only one human being can give to another.

This economy is not new. It is, in fact, the oldest economy in human history: the economy of reciprocal care, mutual aid, and community investment that human beings practiced for most of their time on earth, long before the market economy existed and that has persisted, in the margins and interstices of the market economy, throughout its dominance. What is new is the necessity — in the context of the Identity Crash and the post-utility world — of treating it not as a pleasant supplement to the market economy's forms of value but as a primary source of meaning and identity.

The Micro-Economy of Meaning is built through specific acts. Not grand gestures or heroic interventions, but the accumulated weight of small, consistent, genuine investments in the lives of specific other people. The neighbor who notices that an elderly person has not been seen in several days and goes to check. The colleague who takes the time to genuinely mentor a junior person, not for the credit it generates but because they remember what it meant when someone did it for them. The parent who turns off the screen is genuinely present, with full attention, during the thirty minutes before bedtime. The friend who shows up, without being asked, on the day when showing up is what is needed. The teacher who sees something in a student that the student cannot yet see in themselves and says so, with the specific authority of someone who has genuinely paid attention.

These acts are small in isolation. In aggregate, and over time, they constitute a form of wealth that is both more durable and more genuinely satisfying than any form of market-validated professional achievement. They build what sociologists call social capital: the network of trust, reciprocity, and mutual obligation that is the substrate of genuine community, and that is, according to the research literature on wellbeing, one of the most reliable predictors of both psychological health and physical longevity that exists.

VIII. Building the Micro-Economy: Practical Principles

The Micro-Economy of Meaning does not build itself. It requires deliberate, consistent investment, and it requires a set of orientations and practices that are, in important ways, the opposite of the orientations and practices that the Church of the Grind cultivated. The professional networking culture of the knowledge economy taught people to invest their social energy strategically: to prioritize relationships with high potential for professional return, to manage one's social presence with the same deliberateness one brought to one's personal brand, and to evaluate social investments in terms of their contribution to professional advancement. The Micro-Economy of Meaning requires a fundamentally different orientation: investment in relationships and communities based not on their professional utility but on their genuine human significance.

The first practical principle of building the Micro-Economy is radical specificity: the commitment to genuine investment in specific, known, particular people and communities rather than the broad cultivation of a general social network. The Micro-Economy of Meaning is not built by increasing one's social media following or expanding one's professional contacts. It is built by deepening one's investment in the specific people and places that already constitute one's actual life: the neighbors one has never really spoken to, the community organizations that exist in one's area and that have never seemed worth attending, the old friendships that have faded for no better reason than the mutual busyness of lives organized around professional achievement.

The second practical principle is the priority of presence over performance. The contribution that builds the Micro-Economy is not the impressive contribution — the large donation, the spectacular intervention, the publicly visible act of generosity that generates social recognition and professional goodwill. It is the consistent, present, attentive contribution: the person who shows up reliably, who pays genuine attention to the people around them, who is available when availability is what is needed. Presence is not glamorous. It does not generate the kind of recognition that the Church of the Grind rewarded. But it is, according to everyone who has benefited from it and everyone who has studied human flourishing, the single most important thing that human beings can offer each other.

The third practical principle is what might be called the economy of teaching: the deliberate sharing of one's skills, knowledge, and experience with people who do not yet possess them, not as professional instruction or for financial compensation, but as an expression of the specifically human impulse to transmit what one knows to the people who will carry it forward. The person who teaches a child to read, who shows a young neighbor how to change the oil in a car, who passes on a family recipe with all the accumulated knowledge of its variations and the stories attached to its occasions, who sits with a junior colleague and shares not merely technical knowledge but the harder-won wisdom of professional experience — this person is creating value in the Micro-Economy of Meaning that compounds in ways that financial investments never do.

The reason is simple: human knowledge and skill, when transmitted person-to-person, does not merely transfer from one person to another. It multiplies. The person who learns something does not merely possess what they learned. They become someone who knows this thing, who can use it, who can teach it in turn to someone else, and whose relationship with the person who taught them is permanently enriched by the specific quality of generosity and genuine attention that the teaching represented. This multiplication is the compound interest of the Micro-Economy of Meaning, and it is the reason why the investment of time and skill in genuine human transmission is among the highest-return activities available to a person navigating the post-utility world.

IX. Integration: How the Three Practices Reinforce Each Other

The Deep Hour, the Physical Anchor, and the Micro-Economy of Meaning are not three independent practices that happen to be grouped under a common heading. They are three dimensions of a single integrated approach to living that work together, reinforce each other, and produce effects in combination that none of them produces in isolation. Understanding how they integrate is essential to understanding why the blueprint works and what happens when any one of its three components is absent.

The Deep Hour builds the capacity for sustained, self-directed engagement: the attentional depth, the tolerance for difficulty, and the quality of self-knowledge that comes from regular encounter with demanding analog material. It develops, over time, the specific cognitive and psychological resources that genuine human contribution requires — the ability to think clearly, to see deeply, to bring genuine attention to the things that most require it. Without these resources, the other two practices are impoverished: the Physical Anchor becomes merely physical exercise, disconnected from the self-reflective engagement that gives it its deeper significance, and the Micro-Economy of Meaning becomes superficial, lacking the depth of presence and genuine attention that makes its contributions genuinely valuable.

The Physical Anchor grounds the Deep Hour in the reality of embodied existence: it prevents the self-cultivation of the morning practice from becoming a purely cerebral, disembodied project that floats free of the physical world. It develops the specific form of self-confidence — the trust in one's own body's capacity to meet genuine difficulty — that is one of the most important psychological resources for navigating the Identity Crash. And it provides, through the daily experience of genuine physical effort, a form of reality-testing that the cognitive and social dimensions of the blueprint cannot supply: the unambiguous feedback of a body working at its edge, which cuts through the fog of self-deception and performative busyness with the clarity of genuine physical truth.

The Micro-Economy of Meaning gives the other two practices their larger human purpose. The Deep Hour and the Physical Anchor, practiced in isolation from genuine human connection and contribution, risk becoming forms of self-improvement that serve only the improver: a sophisticated version of the Church of the Grind's self-optimization culture, simply redirected from professional to personal development. The Micro-Economy of Meaning prevents this by embedding the self-development of the other practices in a network of genuine human relationships and obligations: by insisting that the capacities being cultivated are not ends in themselves but resources to be deployed in the service of the people and communities to which one has genuinely committed.

This integration also works in the reverse direction: the genuine human relationships of the Micro-Economy provide the motivation and the context that make the Deep Hour and the Physical Anchor sustainable over the long term. The person who maintains their deep reading practice partly because it makes them a better and more interesting conversation partner for the people they love is more likely to maintain it through the inevitable periods of flagging motivation than the person who maintains it purely for their own self-development. The person whose physical practice is shared with a training partner or a team is more likely to sustain it through illness and weather and the competing demands of a full life than the person who practices alone.

The integrated blueprint is, in this sense, a description of a way of being in the world rather than a set of isolated techniques for self-improvement. It is an architecture for a life that is simultaneously inward-directed — in its cultivation of genuine depth, genuine presence, and genuine self-knowledge — and outward-directed — in its commitment to genuine contribution, genuine community, and genuine care. This integration of the inward and the outward, of self-cultivation and service, is not merely aesthetically satisfying. It is psychologically necessary: the research on human flourishing is consistent that genuine wellbeing requires both genuine engagement with one's own interior life and genuine engagement with the lives of others. Neither alone is sufficient. Together, they constitute the structure of a life that is genuinely worth living.

X. The Blueprint in Time: Patience, Failure, and the Long Game

The post-utility blueprint is not a program that produces results in thirty days. It is not a system that, once installed, runs automatically without continued investment. It is a practice — in the deepest sense of that word, the sense in which musicians practice and athletes practice and meditators practice: a sustained, long-term engagement with a set of activities that develop their full value only through the accumulated weight of consistent effort over months and years.

This is worth stating plainly, because the culture of the Church of the Grind has trained most people to expect rapid, measurable results from any significant investment of time and effort — and to interpret the absence of such results as evidence that the investment is not working and should be abandoned. The Deep Hour and the Physical Anchor and the Micro-Economy of Meaning do not produce rapid, measurable results, and any honest account of what they produce must acknowledge this. What they produce, over time, is a transformation in the quality of one's engagement with existence: a deepening of attention, a strengthening of presence, a growing richness in one's relationships and one's inner life, and a gradually increasing sense of groundedness in one's own values and capacities that is quite different from the professional confidence of the Church of the Grind but more durable.

The timeline of this transformation is, in most people's experience, measured in years rather than months. The first year of the Deep Hour produces primarily the recalibration of the attentional system: the gradual reduction of the Dopamine Trap's hold and the gradual recovery of the capacity for sustained, self-directed engagement. The first year of the Physical Anchor produces primarily the establishment of the practice as a genuine habit and the first evidence of developing physical capacity. The first year of the Micro-Economy of Meaning primarily produces the initial investments in relationships and communities whose return will not be fully apparent for years.

By the third year, something genuinely different has typically emerged: a quality of daily life that is recognizably richer, more grounded, and more genuinely satisfying than the life organized around professional identity and market-validated achievement that preceded it. Not easier — the post-utility life is not easier than the Church of the Grind life. In many respects it is harder, because it demands genuine presence and genuine investment rather than the performance of these qualities. But more real. More fully inhabited. More genuinely one's own.

Failure is an essential component of this process, and any account of the blueprint that omits it is dishonest. The Deep Hour will be missed on days when the demands of life are too pressing. The Physical Anchor will be abandoned during periods of illness, travel, or exceptional stress. The investments in the Micro-Economy of Meaning will sometimes be rejected, unreciprocated, or simply insufficient to the needs of the people they were intended to serve. These failures are not evidence that the blueprint is not working. They are evidence that the blueprint is being practiced by a human being in the actual conditions of a human life, which are always messier, more demanding, and less responsive to deliberate intention than any system of self-improvement can fully account for.

The appropriate response to failure in the practice of the blueprint is not guilt, not extended self-analysis, and not the abandonment of the practice in favor of a newer, more promising system. It is return: the simple, undramatic act of beginning again tomorrow morning. The Deep Hour that was missed yesterday is not a debt to be repaid or a failure to be mourned. It is simply yesterday's practice, and today's practice begins now. This quality of patient, non-judgmental return is not merely a psychological technique for maintaining the practice. It is itself a form of the practice: a daily exercise in the kind of self-compassion, self-knowledge, and honest self-assessment that the post-utility life both requires and develops.

The person who has maintained the blueprint through failure as well as success, through the years of slow transformation as well as the occasional breakthrough, through the quiet Monday mornings when the work seems difficult and unrewarding as well as the luminous days when everything feels clear and purposeful — this person has built something that no disruption of the market, no advancement of artificial intelligence, and no reorganization of the economy can take away. They have built a self: a genuine, grounded, fully inhabited human self that knows what it values, knows what it is capable of, and knows — from the inside, from the accumulated evidence of years of honest practice — that it is enough.

The blueprint is not the destination. It is the daily act of becoming adequate to the life that is waiting.

CHAPTER EIGHT

NAVIGATING THE TRANSITION

✦ ✦ ✦

I. THE SPACE BETWEEN

The great danger of any book about transformation is that it might make the process sound tidier than it is. The preceding chapters have offered a diagnosis of the Identity Crash, a map of its specific pathologies, and an architecture for the life that becomes possible on the other side of it. What they cannot fully convey — what no amount of clear analysis can adequately prepare a person for — is the experience of being in the middle of the transition itself. Not before it has begun, and not after you have emerged from it with a new framework for living, but in the actual, disorienting, unglamorous middle of it.

This chapter is about that middle. It is about the specific psychological, social, and practical challenges of the transitional period — the weeks, months, and sometimes years during which the old identity has been sufficiently disrupted to make the old ways of living feel inadequate, but the new identity has not yet solidified sufficiently to provide reliable guidance and stable ground. This period is not a failure state. It is not evidence that the transition is going badly. It is, in fact, the most important and in some respects the most generative phase of the entire process. But it is also the phase during which most people either make genuine progress or quietly retreat into the familiar pathologies of the old framework, because the discomfort of the middle is so much more immediately present than the promise of the other side.

William Bridges, whose work on life transitions remains among the most useful available, distinguished between the external change that initiates a transition and the internal psychological process the transition requires. External changes — the job restructuring, the role automation, the professional displacement — happen to us, often without our consent. The internal transition — the psychological journey from the identity organized around the old professional self to the identity organized around something more durable and more genuinely human — is something we must actively undertake. And it has a structure: an ending phase in which the old identity is released, a neutral zone in which nothing stable has yet replaced it, and a new beginning in which a different and more grounded way of being starts to coalesce.

The neutral zone is the hardest part. Bridges described it as a time of confusion, disorientation, and apparent purposelessness — a time when the person has let go of who they were but has not yet become who they are becoming. It is characterized by a specific quality of psychological emptiness that is neither the grief of ending nor the hope of beginning, but something more ambiguous and more difficult to hold: the experience of being between stories, without the comfort of either the old narrative or a fully articulated new one.

This book calls that neutral zone the transition, and this chapter is its map. Not a map that eliminates the disorientation — the disorientation is real and cannot be eliminated, only navigated. But a map that names the specific features of the terrain, identifies the most significant hazards, and points toward the resources that are genuinely available to the person who is willing to engage with the process rather than flee from it.

II. The Grief Nobody Names

The first and most important thing to understand about navigating the transition is that it requires genuine grief. Not the metaphorical grief of self-help rhetoric — "mourn the old you and embrace the new!" — but actual, serious grief. The kind that arrives uninvited at odd moments, that has no decorum about its timing, that resists the reassurances of well-meaning friends who tell you that things will work out and that you are going to be fine.

This grief is appropriate, and it should be taken seriously rather than managed away. The loss that grief is responding to is real. The skills you spent years developing, the expertise that defined your professional identity, the quality of focused engagement that characterized your best work — these were genuine goods. They had value. They gave your days a shape and a purpose that was not anything, even if the Church of the Grind inflated their importance in ways that were psychologically costly. The fact that their market value has been disrupted does not retroactively erase the genuine worth they had, or the genuine investment of self that went into their development.

Allowing yourself to grieve this loss is not self-indulgence. It is a prerequisite for genuine forward movement. The research on major life transitions is consistent on this point: the people who move through them most successfully are not those who suppress or bypass the grief, but those who engage with it honestly, allow it to run its full course, and integrate it into a more complete understanding of what has changed and what has not. The person who jumps immediately to "upskilling" or "pivoting" without first sitting with the loss tends to find themselves, months or years later, experiencing the grief they bypassed — often at a moment when it is far more disruptive to do so.

The grief of the Identity Crash has several specific dimensions that are worth naming separately, because each requires a different quality of attention.

The first is the grief of lost mastery. The skills you developed over years of deliberate practice — the specific, finely tuned cognitive competencies that made you genuinely excellent at something genuinely difficult — were a form of self-expression as much as a professional asset. When those skills are rendered economically redundant by automation, what is lost is not merely a job function. It is a specific way of being excellent in the world — a channel through which intelligence, care, and genuine effort found expression in things that mattered to other people. This loss has aesthetic as well as economic dimensions. It deserves to be mourned as such.

The second is the grief of lost identity. For most knowledge workers, professional identity is not merely a label. It is a story — a narrative of how one's unique combination of skills, experiences, and judgment found its appropriate expression in a specific professional role. The legal mind. The clinical eye. The strategic thinker. The creative director. These are not simply job titles. They are character descriptions: ways of understanding oneself as a particular kind of person with a particular kind of contribution to make to the world. When the economic foundations of that character description erode, the loss is not merely external. It is the loss of a particular story about who one is. And stories about who we are not easily or painlessly surrendered.

The third is the grief of lost community. The workplace, whatever its frustrations, provides for most people the most consistently available structure of social belonging in their adult lives. The colleagues, the shared projects, the daily rhythms of professional interaction — these constitute, for many people, the primary social context within which they feel genuinely known, genuinely competent, and genuinely connected to something larger than their own private existence. When the professional role erodes — when the ghost employment becomes undeniable, or when the retraining or restructuring is complete and one finds oneself in a genuinely different professional context — this community is often disrupted or lost entirely. The grief of this loss is frequently underacknowledged because it is mixed up with the other dimensions of the transition and because there is no conventional social ritual for mourning the end of a professional community.

III. The Identity Inventory: Recovering the Submerged Self

One of the most useful practices available to someone in the middle of the transition is what the book has called the Identity Inventory: a deliberate, unhurried examination of the multiple sources of identity, connection, and meaning that a person's life contains — as opposed to the ones that their professional role has trained them to emphasize.

The Identity Inventory begins with a disarmingly simple question: If I could not describe myself by my job title, how would I describe myself? The first attempts at answering this question often produce a kind of blank — the psychological equivalent of trying to see a room after the lights have suddenly gone out. The professional identity has been so central, for so long, that the other sources of identity have atrophied through disuse, or retreated so far into the background of daily life that they are no longer easily accessible to conscious reflection.

But they are there. They are always there. They include the roles one plays in one's close relationships: the parent, the partner, the friend, the sibling, the neighbor. They include the passions and interests that have survived the depredations of the Grind, however attenuated: the person who loves gardening, who reads history compulsively, who has always had a feeling for music, who finds themselves most alive when they are moving their body in challenging physical activity. They include the values that have guided consequential choices, even when those choices were costly: the commitment to honesty, the care for the vulnerable, the drive toward beauty, the refusal of certain kinds of compromise.

The Identity Inventory is not a one-time exercise. It is a practice — something to be returned to, refined, and deepened over time. The first session will typically produce a thin account, because the habit of seeing oneself primarily through the professional lens is deeply ingrained and does not dissolve in a single sitting. But with each return to the exercise — each fresh attempt to describe oneself honestly in terms that are not borrowed from the job description — the account grows richer and more complex. The person begins to see themselves as a more dimensional creature than the job title suggested. They begin to recover access to aspects of themselves that the professional identity had not merely marginalized but suppressed: the curiosity that was always broader than any single field of expertise; the care for other people that was always more expansive than any client relationship; the aesthetic sensibility that was always seeking expression beyond the professional outputs it was enlisted to serve.

The practice of the Identity Inventory has a specific neurological dimension that is worth noting. The default mode network — the brain's self-referential processing system, described in the chapter on the Dopamine Trap — is the primary neural substrate of autobiographical self-reflection: the process by which we integrate our experiences, values, and commitments into a coherent sense of who we are over time. When that network is perpetually suppressed by the demands of professional activity and the stimulation of the digital environment, the self that it constructs remains impoverished and one-dimensional. The Identity Inventory, by deliberately creating the conditions for sustained, undirected self-reflection, activates the default mode network in ways that make the recovery of the submerged self not merely possible but neurologically inevitable.

The key is time: sufficient, unhurried, uninterrupted time to sit with the questions without rushing to answers. Not the twenty-minute lunch break or the stolen ten minutes before sleep. Real time: an hour or two, in a quiet place, with a notebook, a pen, and the willingness to write honestly about what is there when you look.

IV. The Neutral Zone: What to Do When Nothing is Settled

The neutral zone — the period between the dissolution of the old identity and the consolidation of the new one — has a characteristic phenomenology that is worth describing in some detail, because recognizing it for what it is can make the difference between engaging with it productively and fleeing from it into one of the familiar escape routes that the Dopamine Trap and the residual Church of the Grind provide.

The neutral zone feels like failure, but it is not failure. It feels like emptiness, but the emptiness is generative. It feels like being lost, but being lost in this specific way — having genuinely released the old framework without yet having arrived at the new one — is a precondition for the kind of genuine discovery that a more comfortable position does not permit. You cannot find new ground while you are still standing on the old ground. The disorientation of the neutral zone is the price of the genuine openness that makes the new beginning possible.

The primary psychological task of the neutral zone is not to resolve the uncertainty as quickly as possible. It is to develop a capacity to inhabit uncertainty without being destroyed by it — to cultivate what the poet John Keats called "negative capability": the ability to remain in doubt and uncertainty without an irritable reaching after fact and reason. This is not a passive or comfortable state. It is an active, sustained practice of holding the questions open while resisting the premature closure that the mind — trained by the Church of the Grind to resolve every problem into actionable steps and measurable outcomes — perpetually reaches for.

In practice, the neutral zone is navigated most successfully by a combination of two complementary orientations. The first is orientation toward structure: maintaining the daily practices — the Deep Hour, the Physical Anchor, the investments in the Micro-Economy of Meaning — that provide a reliable architecture of engagement even when the larger questions of professional identity and direction remain unresolved. The person in the neutral zone who maintains these practices is not merely killing time until the transition resolves. They are actively building the capacities and relationships that the new beginning will require, and they are doing so in a way that provides the daily experience of genuine engagement, genuine challenge, and genuine connection that makes the uncertainty of the neutral zone psychologically survivable.

The second orientation is toward openness: a deliberate, practiced willingness to encounter experiences, people, and ideas that would not have been part of the old professional identity's territory. The neutral zone is, among other things, a period of maximum creative possibility: the old framework no longer constrains what you can be interested in, what you can try, what you can allow to matter to you. The person who uses this period to follow genuine curiosity wherever it leads — to take the class in something they always found interesting but professionally irrelevant, to engage with the community organization they always drove past, to have the conversation with the person whose life looks nothing like the life they had planned — will find that the neutral zone is not merely an uncomfortable passage but a genuinely generative period of discovery.

V. The Re-Entry Problem: Social Navigation in the In-Between

One of the most disorienting experiences of the Identity Crash's transitional period is what might be called the Re-Entry Problem: the difficulty of engaging authentically with social and professional environments that are still operating according to the old framework, at a time when you have already begun to move beyond it.

The Re-Entry Problem manifests most acutely in social situations organized around the conventions of professional identity. You are at a dinner party, a family gathering, a networking event, a school reunion. Someone asks, "What do you do?" In the old world — the world of stable professional identity and clear market-valued contribution — this question had a clear, comfortable, and socially legible answer. In the in-between world of the transition, the answer is suddenly complicated. You may still hold the same job title, while knowing privately that its content has been hollowed out. You may have left a previous role and not yet settled into a new one. You may have undergone the interior transformation described in this book to a degree that makes the old answer feel dishonest, without having found a new answer that is both accurate and socially navigable.

The discomfort this creates is not trivial. Human beings are deeply social creatures, and the experience of not being able to account for oneself in terms that one's social environment can recognize and accept is a genuinely distressing one. The professional identity — whatever its limitations as a foundation for genuine selfhood — had the undeniable social virtue of legibility. People knew how to place you. You knew how to place yourself. The transaction was smooth, comfortable, and invisible in its efficiency. The absence of that efficiency — the sudden awkwardness of the "What do you do?" question — is one of the most consistently reported features of the transitional experience.

There is no universally correct answer to the Re-Entry Problem. But there is a useful reframe that many people find helpful: the question "What do you do?" is a social convention, not an existential inquiry. Its function is to establish a shared context for conversation, to signal mutual recognition, and to initiate the process of finding common ground with a new acquaintance. It is not — or should not be — a demand for a complete accounting of one's worth, purpose, and self-concept. You can satisfy its social function without submitting to the ontological claim that lurks behind it: that what you do professionally is the most important and interesting thing about you.

Learning to answer, "What do you do?" with something authentic that is not merely a job title is a small act of cultural subversion with consequences that extend well beyond the individual conversation. It is a practice of inhabiting, in public, the larger and more genuine identity that the transition is demanding you develop. And it is a practice that, over time, trains both the practitioner and the people around them to recognize that the most interesting thing about a person is rarely captured in a job description.

The Re-Entry Problem also manifests in professional contexts: the team meeting in which everyone is performing the rituals of professional engagement with an earnestness that you can no longer entirely share; the performance review in which you must account for your contributions in terms that no longer capture what you believe your genuine contributions actually are; the networking event at which the exchange of professional credentials and aspirations feels increasingly hollow against the backdrop of the more genuine forms of connection you are beginning to cultivate elsewhere. In each of these contexts, the challenge is to maintain sufficient professional engagement to honor the genuine obligations of your role while simultaneously beginning the quiet, private work of building the new identity that the transition requires.

VI. The Importance of Witnesses

One of the most consistent findings in the research literature on major life transitions is the importance of what sociologists call "bridging relationships": relationships with people who know both who you were and who you are becoming, who can hold both versions of you in their awareness without requiring you to be one or the other, and who are genuinely interested in the process rather than merely in the outcome.

These relationships are rare, and their rarity is one of the most significant practical challenges of the transitional period. Most of our social relationships are organized around shared context and shared identity — the colleagues who know us as the professional we are currently transitioning away from, the family members who relate to us in terms of the roles we have occupied for decades, the friends whose friendship was initiated and maintained in the context of the professional and social world of the old identity. These are not bad relationships. They are often deeply important ones. But they are not, in most cases, well positioned to serve the specific function that the transition requires.

A witness, in the sense relevant here, is something more specific than a supportive friend or a sympathetic colleague. A witness is someone who can hold the full complexity of your transitional experience without simplifying it into either reassurance or alarm. Someone who is genuinely interested in the process, not merely in the outcome. Someone who will ask, "How is this going for you?" and want to hear the complicated answer — not the socially appropriate answer, not the optimistic answer that protects their comfort, but the actual answer, with its ambiguities and confusions and occasional moments of genuine discovery. Someone who will not be disappointed or alarmed by the setbacks and the confusion that are an inevitable part of genuine transition.

Where are witnesses found? In some cases, they already exist in one's life: the old friend who has always had an unusual capacity for genuine conversation; the therapist or coach who has been trained specifically to accompany people through difficult transitions; the mentor whose own life has included enough genuine transition that they recognize the terrain and can navigate it without panic. In other cases, they must be found or created: through the kind of genuine community building described in the chapter on the Micro-Economy of Meaning; through the support groups and transition communities that are beginning to emerge around the specific experience of professional displacement in the age of AI; through the deliberate cultivation of relationships with people who are navigating the same transition and who have, therefore, the specific kind of experiential knowledge that no amount of theoretical understanding can substitute for.

The value of witnesses cannot be overstated. Human beings do not navigate major identity transitions well in isolation. We are, in the most fundamental sense, social creatures: our self-understanding is constructed in relationship, our capacity for honest self-examination is supported by the presence of others who can reflect what they see, and our resilience in the face of difficulty is sustained by the knowledge that we are not alone in our struggle. The person who attempts to navigate the Identity Crash entirely in private — maintaining a professional front in all external contexts while processing the transition alone, in the silence of their own interior — is carrying a burden that does not need to be, and should not be, carried alone.

VII. Redefining Success: New Metrics for an Unmeasured Life

One of the most difficult practical challenges of the transitional period is the development of new metrics for success — new ways of evaluating whether a day, a week, a month, a year has gone well. The old metrics were simple, if brutal: productivity, output, advancement, income. These metrics had the virtue of clarity. They were legible, comparable, and socially recognized. When you met them, you knew you had met them. When you fell short, there was no ambiguity about the shortfall.

The new metrics are more complex, more subjective, and more resistant to easy quantification. They require a different relationship with evaluation itself: a willingness to live, at least in part, in the unmeasured dimensions of experience, and to trust that the quality of one's engagement with those dimensions is real and important even when it resists the clean accounting of a performance dashboard.

The new metrics might include: the quality of attention you brought to your most important relationships today. The depth of engagement you experienced during your Deep Hour. The degree to which you felt genuinely present in your own life, rather than merely passing through it on the way to the next task. The number of moments in which you contributed something genuine to another person's day — not a transaction, not a service delivery, but a genuine act of attention, care, or presence that made a real difference to a specific human being. The degree to which the choices you made today were consistent with the values you identified in your Identity Inventory, as opposed to the reflexive responses of the professional self-concept that the transition is gradually releasing.

These metrics will feel inadequate, initially, to the person who has spent years in the clear and bracing air of quantifiable achievement. They will feel soft, subjective, and not serious enough to carry the weight of a life's evaluation. This feeling is accurate: they are softer, more subjective, and more difficult to defend in the social contexts that the Church of the Grind organized. But they are not less serious. They are, in fact, more accurate measures of the things that determine the quality of a life — more aligned with what the research on human flourishing consistently identifies as the genuine predictors of sustained wellbeing and genuine satisfaction.

The transition from old metrics to new ones is not accomplished in a single decision or a single conversation with oneself. It is a gradual recalibration, accomplished through the accumulation of days in which one deliberately evaluates one's experience according to the new framework rather than the old one — and gradually discovers, as the recalibration proceeds, that the new framework is not a consolation prize but a more adequate account of what matters in a human life.

VIII. The Accelerator, the Avoider, and the Others: Recognizing Yourself in the Transition

The transitional experience of the Identity Crash does not produce a uniform psychological response. It manifests differently depending on personality, professional context, the degree to which professional identity has been fused with self-concept, and the specific nature and pace of the disruption being experienced. Recognizing one's own characteristic response to the transition is a crucial step in navigating it, because each response pattern carries its own specific hazards that are difficult to see from inside the pattern.

The Accelerator is the person who responds to the threat of displacement by working harder, faster, and more obsessively than ever before. They are easy to miss as someone in distress because their distress is entirely invisible beneath the hyperactivity it produces. They are first in the office and last to leave. They respond to emails at midnight. They volunteer for additional responsibilities, take on more projects than any human being can complete with genuine engagement, and maintain an appearance of extraordinary professional dedication that serves, primarily, as a screen against the recognition that the genuine substance of the work has migrated elsewhere. The Accelerator is not lazy. They are terrified. And their terror has taken the form of a productivity that is, paradoxically, the most efficient path to the burnout that will eventually force the reckoning they have been fleeing.

The Avoider is in many respects the mirror image of the Accelerator. Where the Accelerator responds to threat by doing more, the Avoider responds by doing less progressively. They procrastinate, defer decisions, find elaborate reasons why the project is not yet ready to begin, why the conversation is not yet the right moment to have, why the transition cannot really begin until some specific external condition has been met. Their avoidance is not laziness — it is, at a deeper level, a refusal to produce evidence that can be judged. If they never finish the report, no AI can be set alongside it as a more efficient alternative. If they never complete their career pivot, it can never be found wanting. The Avoider is protecting the last refuge of the Uselessness Syndrome: the possibility, still intact as long as the work remains undone, that they might be excellent.

The Nostalgist has not lost the capacity to work effectively; they have lost the desire. They remember vividly a time when the work felt different — when the effort required felt proportionate to the significance of the output, when the gap between the work and the tool was not so vast, when professional identity felt like an earned and genuine expression of genuine capacity. They speak often of how things used to be, how craftsmanship used to matter, how the profession used to require something that it no longer seems to require. Their grief is real and legitimate. But it has calcified into a posture of retrospective idealization that is preventing them from engaging honestly with the genuine possibilities — genuinely different, genuinely demanding, but genuinely available — of the present moment.

The Philosopher has arrived, often through genuine pain, at a kind of intellectual detachment from the domain of professional identity. They speak about the disruption with equanimity, sometimes with wry amusement. They quote thinkers. They seem, in conversations about the future of work, to be the calmest person in the room. What they often cannot admit — sometimes even to themselves — is that the detachment is not genuine philosophical serenity. It is a defense mechanism: a way of ensuring that what they care about can no longer hurt them, by the simple expedient of pretending they no longer care. The Philosopher needs not more philosophy but more honest contact with the specific, concrete, particular grief that the philosophical posture is managing at arm's length.

Recognizing oneself in one of these patterns is not a cause for shame. It is information: a signal about the specific form that the transition's challenges are taking in one's own experience, and therefore about the specific interventions that are most likely to be genuinely helpful. The Accelerator needs rest and honest reckoning. The Avoider needs structure and the support of witnesses who can accompany them into the work they have been avoiding. The Nostalgist needs the space to grieve fully before being asked to engage with the present. The Philosopher needs the courage to feel what they have been thinking about.

IX. The Body in Transition: Why the Physical Matters So Much

One of the most consistent and least well-understood findings about major life transitions is the degree to which they are experienced in the body rather than merely in the mind. The disorientation, the fatigue, the disruption of sleep, the loss of appetite or the compulsive eating, the physical heaviness that accompanies genuine grief, the specific tension that settles in the shoulders and the jaw during sustained periods of professional anxiety — these are not merely metaphors for psychological states. They are the psychological states, expressed in their primary medium: the living body.

This is why the Physical Anchor — described in Chapter Seven as one of the three foundational practices of the post-utility blueprint — is particularly important during the transitional period rather than merely in the stable post-transition life. The body in transition is under specific and sustained physiological stress. The chronic activation of the threat-response systems — the cortisol elevation, the sympathetic nervous system arousal, the suppression of the parasympathetic rest-and-digest state — that characterizes the experience of sustained identity threat produces real and measurable physiological consequences: disrupted sleep, impaired immune function, increased inflammation, reduced cognitive flexibility and executive function.

Regular vigorous physical activity is one of the most effective available interventions for all these consequences. It down-regulates the cortisol response, activates the parasympathetic nervous system, promotes the release of BDNF and other neurotrophic factors that support the neural plasticity necessary for genuine cognitive adaptation, and provides, through the specific experience of physical challenge genuinely met, the daily evidence of personal efficacy that the erosion of professional identity threatens to eliminate. The person in transition who maintains a serious physical practice is not merely staying healthy. They are maintaining the neurological and psychological conditions under which genuine transition can occur.

The physical dimension of transition has a deeper significance beyond its neurological benefits, however. Major identity transitions require, at some level, a reorientation of one's entire relationship to one's own existence — a shift in the center of gravity of one's sense of self from the professional-cognitive domain to something more fundamental. And the most fundamental thing available to a human being — the thing that is present before any professional identity and after any professional identity has dissolved — is the body. The physical self. The breathing, moving, feeling organism that is the substrate and the source of everything else that one is.

The person who, during the most disorienting phase of the transition, can come home to their body — who can find in the daily practice of physical challenge a form of identity and engagement that is impervious to the disruptions of the knowledge economy and immune to the assessments of the market — has access to a resource that no algorithm can compete with and no organizational restructuring can take away. The body is always there. It is always yours. In the transition, as in everything else, it is the ground you are standing on.

X. The Other Side: What Genuine Transition Produces

The transitional period ends — not with a dramatic revelation or a clean resolution, but with the gradual emergence of a different quality of experience: a growing sense of groundedness that is not dependent on external validation, a capacity to engage with the specific conditions of one's life — whatever those conditions are — with something closer to genuine equanimity than to the performed equanimity of the Philosopher, and an increasing recognition that the identity being constructed on the other side of the transition is, in some essential respect, more genuinely one's own than the identity it replaced.

This recognition has a specific phenomenological quality that is difficult to describe but reliably recognized by those who have experienced it: a quality of coming home. Not to a previous version of the self — the transition produces genuine change, and the person who emerges from it is not the same person who entered it. But to something that was always present beneath the professional persona, beneath the performative competence, beneath the identity organized around productive utility and market validation. To the self that was there before the Church of the Grind told it what it was supposed to be.

People who have successfully navigated the transition consistently report several specific changes in the texture of their daily experience. The first is a changed relationship with time: a reduction in the chronic sense of urgency — the perpetual experience of being behind, of never doing enough, of time as a resource that is always being depleted faster than it can be replenished — and its replacement with a more spacious relationship with the present moment. The work is still important. The relationships are still demanding. The life is still full. But the quality of engagement with it is different: more present, more patient, more genuinely inhabiting the specific moment rather than perpetually racing toward the next one.

The second is a changed relationship with failure. The person who has successfully decoupled their sense of worth from their professional performance discovers that failure — the inevitable, recurring, genuinely instructive failures of anyone who is engaged with difficult and genuinely uncertain work — no longer carries the existential charge it once did. It is still uncomfortable. It still requires honest examination and genuine effort to understand and address. But it is no longer a threat to the self because the self is no longer housed primarily in the performance domain where the failure occurred. The failure is information. It is not a verdict.

The third is a changed relationship with other people: specifically, a deeper capacity for genuine presence in relationship. The person who is no longer primarily concerned with how the relationship is serving their professional identity, or what the other person thinks of their professional accomplishments, or whether the interaction is productive and efficient enough to justify the time it requires, is a person who is available for the kind of genuine, unhurried, mutually interested human connection that constitutes the most reliable source of sustained wellbeing that research has identified. The transition, in dissolving the professional self's dominance over the field of attention, makes space for a quality of relational presence that was always possible but rarely practiced.

None of this is permanent. The old habits of mind reassert themselves, especially in professional contexts that still organize themselves around the old framework. The comparison anxiety returns. The performance orientation resurfaces. The impulse to measure oneself against the old metrics persists. The transition is not a one-time event from which one emerges permanently transformed. It is a direction of travel, maintained through practice, through honest self-examination, and through the daily choices about how to orient one's attention and engage one's capacity.

But the direction is real. And the person who has genuinely engaged with the transition — who has grieved what was lost, recovered what was submerged, practiced the patience of the neutral zone, built the structures of the post-utility life, and found the witnesses who could accompany the process — is traveling in a direction that no disruption of the market, no advancement of artificial intelligence, and no restructuring of the economy can reverse. They are traveling toward themselves. And the destination, it turns out, is worth the journey.

The transition is not the gap between who you were and who you will be.
It is the most honest encounter with who you are.

CHAPTER NINE

THE NEW PROFESSIONS OF MEANING

✦ ✦ ✦

In the previous chapters, we have spoken mostly about the interior work of the Identity Crash — the psychological, philosophical, and existential dimensions of what it means to reimagine your relationship to your own worth. We have traced how labor became identity, how automation is dissolving that identity, and how the ground of genuine human value — embodiment, irrationality, empathy, presence — has always been richer than the narrow metric of productivity ever acknowledged.

But there is an exterior dimension as well: the practical question of what kinds of work will be available to human beings in the years and decades ahead. What will people do? For what will they be paid? How will the economy of the future distribute the rewards of a world in which machines handle an increasing proportion of cognitive labor? And — most important — how do we build lives around work that is genuinely worth doing, rather than merely economically necessary?

These are not merely economic questions. They are questions about the social organization of meaning — about how human beings will structure their time and their contributions in a world where the traditional structures of employment, career, and professional identity are being fundamentally transformed. They are questions about dignity: about what it means to earn your place in the world through the specific quality of what only you can bring. And they are questions about the future of human community: about what binds us together, what we owe each other, and what kinds of work create the social fabric that makes a civilization genuinely worth inhabiting.

This chapter attempts to sketch, with appropriate humility about the limits of prediction, the broad contours of what human work might look like on the other side of the Efficiency Wall. It does not offer a comprehensive economic forecast or a job-by-job analysis of automation risk. Those analyses exist, and they are valuable. What this chapter offers instead is something different: a map of the domains in which human contribution will be most irreplaceable, most valuable, and most deeply aligned with what it means to live a fully human life. These are the New Professions of Meaning — not replacements for the work that AI is absorbing, but revelations of what was always most important about human work, now made visible by the contrast with what machines can and cannot do.

I. The Persistence of Human Judgment

The first and most important thing to understand about the future of human work is that the elimination of cognitive labor does not mean the elimination of human judgment. Quite the contrary: as the production of cognitive outputs is automated, the demand for human judgment about what those outputs should be used for — and how they should be deployed — is likely to increase substantially.

This distinction — between cognitive output and human judgment — is one of the most important that this book makes, and it deserves careful unpacking. Cognitive output is the product of information processing: the analysis, the diagnosis, the legal brief, the financial model, the software module. These are things that AI systems can now produce with extraordinary speed and, in many domains, with accuracy that rivals or exceeds that of expert human practitioners. Human judgment, by contrast, is the capacity to decide what to do with those outputs — to determine their relevance, their adequacy, their ethical implications, and their fit with the specific human situation in which they are being deployed.

An AI system can tell you, with high confidence, what the optimal investment strategy is given a specific set of financial goals and constraints.

It cannot tell you whether those financial goals are the right ones — whether the pursuit of maximum returns is serving the deeper interests of the person or family in question, whether there are values and relationships that the financial model is failing to capture, whether the person sitting across from you is experiencing a crisis that is distorting their stated preferences in ways that will lead to regret. These are not questions that can be answered by processing more data. They are questions that require a human being who is genuinely present, genuinely curious, and genuinely committed to the wellbeing of the person they are serving.

The Counselor-Professional: Law, Medicine, Finance

Consider the legal profession in detail because it illustrates the transformation with clarity. AI systems can now draft contracts, research case law, identify relevant precedents, and produce legal briefs of professional quality in minutes. These capabilities do not eliminate the need for lawyers. They transform what lawyers are for. The lawyer of the near future will not be primarily a drafter of documents or a researcher of law — these tasks will be handled by AI systems with increasing efficiency and accuracy. The lawyer will be a counselor: someone who helps clients understand not just what the law says, but what it means for their specific situation, what their genuine interests are, and what course of action will serve those interests over the long term.

This kind of counseling requires exactly the capacities that AI systems currently lack: genuine empathy, the ability to read a person's emotional state and adjust one's approach accordingly, the wisdom that comes from years of watching how legal decisions play out in real human lives, and the ethical judgment to advise clients not just on what they can do but on what they should do. A client facing a contentious divorce doesn't just need to know what the law permits. They need someone who can help them understand the difference between what they want right now — in the grip of hurt and anger — and what will serve them and their children in the years ahead. They need someone who has seen this situation before, who knows that the most aggressive legal strategy is often not the wisest one, and who is willing to say so even when the client is paying for aggression.

These are not skills that can be trained in a few weeks or replicated by a sufficiently large dataset. They are, in the deepest sense, human — grounded in the practitioner's own experience of loss, conflict, and the slow education of empathy that a genuinely engaged life provides.

The same transformation is underway in medicine. The physician of the near future will spend less time diagnosing — AI systems increasingly handle the pattern recognition that diagnosis requires, often with greater sensitivity and specificity than human clinicians. The physician will spend more time with the patient as a person: understanding the context of their illness, communicating difficult information with compassion and clarity, navigating the complex emotional and relational dimensions of serious disease, and helping patients make decisions that honor not just their medical prognosis but their values, their relationships, and their vision of what a good life looks like for them.

The same is true in financial advising, in architecture, in engineering, in every domain of professional practice. The specific technical content of professional expertise is being absorbed by AI systems. What remains — what is, in fact, becoming more rather than less valuable — is the human dimension of professional practice: the relationship between practitioner and client, the exercise of judgment in complex and ambiguous situations, the integration of technical knowledge with ethical values and contextual wisdom.

THE ETHICAL NAVIGATOR

Closely related to the counselor-professional is a role that does not yet have a widely recognized name but whose importance is becoming increasingly clear: the Ethical Navigator. This is the person — within an organization, a profession, or a community — whose primary function is to ensure that the deployment of powerful automated systems remains accountable to human values, human interests, and human flourishing.

The Ethical Navigator is not a philosopher in the academic sense, though philosophical training is highly relevant to the role. They are a practical reasoner — someone who can move between the technical realities of what automated systems can and cannot do, the organizational pressures that shape how those systems are deployed, and the human interests that are affected by those deployments. They ask the questions that purely technical or purely commercial analysis leaves out: Who is harmed by this system's errors? Whose interests does it serve and whose does it ignore? What happens to the people who fall outside the distribution on which this model was trained? Is the efficiency we are gaining worth the human cost we are incurring?

These are not questions with algorithmic answers. They are questions that require exactly the kind of wisdom, empathy, and ethical reasoning that the Identity Crash is pushing human beings to develop. And as AI systems become more powerful and more consequential, the Ethical Navigator becomes not a luxury but a necessity — the guardian of the human values that automated systems, however sophisticated, cannot protect on their own.

II. The Care Economy and Its Coming Elevation

The most rapidly growing sector of human employment in the age of intelligent machines is likely to be what economists call the care economy: the vast range of human activities devoted to the wellbeing of other human beings. Healthcare beyond diagnosis and treatment protocol, elder care, childcare, mental health support, special education, community development, social work, chaplaincy, coaching, mentorship — these are the activities that require, at their core, the presence of a human being who genuinely cares about the person they are serving.

The care economy has historically been one of the most undervalued sectors of human activity, both economically and culturally. The 'caring professions' — nursing, teaching, social work, childcare — have been systematically paid less than professions whose outputs are more easily quantified, despite providing services that are, by any reasonable measure, at least as important. Part of this undervaluation has been driven by gender: caring work has been, in the most literal sense, women's work for most of human history, and the devaluation of women's labor has been a persistent feature of industrial-era economies. Part of it has been driven by the ideology of the market, which struggles to price things that are not easily standardized or scaled.

The age of AI offers an opportunity — not a guarantee, but a genuine opportunity — to reverse this long-standing inequity. As the cognitive tasks that have commanded premium wages in the knowledge economy are absorbed by automated systems, the caring tasks that AI cannot perform are left as the primary locus of specifically human economic contribution. The economic logic is shifting. And if societies can translate this shift in the actual structure of human value into an equivalent shift in compensation and cultural status, the care economy could become not merely a refuge for the cognitively displaced but a genuine center of social gravity — the domain around which much of human economic life reorganizes itself.

The Grief of Being Cared For by a Machine

To understand why the care economy is irreplaceable, it is worth sitting with a specific experience that more people are beginning to have: the grief of being cared for by a machine.

This grief is subtle and easy to dismiss, especially in a culture that valorizes efficiency and tends to treat emotional responses to technology as mere sentimentality. But it is real, and it points to something important about the nature of care.

Imagine receiving, from an AI-powered mental health application, a response to a moment of acute distress that is, by all measurable criteria, perfectly calibrated — empathetic in tone, accurate in its identification of your emotional state, thoughtful in its suggested coping strategies, and consistent in its availability. Now imagine receiving, instead, phone calls from friends who have their own problems, their own tiredness, their own limited capacity, but they call because they noticed you seemed off and wanted to check in. The friend's response may be less technically perfect. They may say the wrong thing. They may be distracted by their own worries. But what they offer — what the machine categorically cannot offer — is the fact of their choosing. They chose to call. The choice cost them something. And in the act of choosing, they said something that no algorithm can say: you matter enough to me that I am here, even when it is inconvenient, even when I have nothing useful to give.

This is the irreducible core of care: not the provision of optimal responses, but the act of commitment. The willingness to be inconvenienced by another person's need. The choice to remain present in the face of suffering that you cannot fix. These are things that only a being with genuine agency — a being for whom presence is a choice and not a default — can offer. And they are things for which there is no substitute.

Mental Health and the Hunger for Presence

Nowhere is the irreplaceability of human care more evident than in the domain of mental health, where the global crisis of loneliness, anxiety, and depression is colliding with a severe shortage of trained practitioners and a proliferating array of AI-powered 'mental health' applications.

These applications are not without value. For people with no access to professional care, for people managing mild symptoms who need support between sessions, for people who are not yet ready to engage with a human practitioner — AI-powered tools can provide real benefit. They can offer evidence-based coping strategies, psychoeducation, crisis resources, and a degree of availability that human practitioners cannot match. This is not anything.

But the research is consistent: the single most important predictor of positive outcomes in psychotherapy is not the specific technique employed, nor the theoretical orientation of the practitioner, nor the evidence-based protocol being followed. It is the quality of the therapeutic relationship — the degree to which the client experiences themselves as genuinely known, genuinely accepted, and genuinely accompanied by another human being. This 'therapeutic alliance' is not something that can be engineered by optimizing an algorithm's responses. It emerges from the encounter between two conscious beings, one of whom has made a specific, costly commitment to the other.

The mental health professional of the post-AI era will not be replaced by technology. They will, if the transition goes well, be freed from the purely informational dimensions of their work — the psychoeducation that can be delivered more efficiently by an app, the routine monitoring that can be automated — and enabled to focus on what only they can provide: the full quality of their human presence, their capacity for genuine relationship, their willingness to be moved, disturbed, and challenged by the lives of the people they serve. This is harder work, not easier. It requires more of the practitioner, not less. But it is also more valuable, more meaningful, and more effective.

Elder Care: The Ethical Frontier

If mental health care represents one frontier of the care economy's expansion, elder care represents another — and in some ways a more urgent one. The aging of populations across the developed world, combined with declining birth rates and the dissolution of extended family structures that once distributed the labor of elder care across communities, has created a care deficit that is already severe and will become dramatically more severe in the decades ahead.

AI and robotics are being developed to address this deficit, and they will provide genuine assistance — with medication management, with mobility support, with cognitive monitoring, with the reduction of certain kinds of isolation. An elderly person with a companion robot is better off than an elderly person with no company at all. The data on this is clear.

But the data is equally clear that what elderly people most need — and most consistently report as missing from their lives — is not better medication management or more efficient monitoring. It is genuine human connection. The experience of being known by name, remembered across conversations, treated as a person with a history and a perspective rather than a patient with a set of conditions. The experience of being touched — not just managed — by hands that carry the warmth of genuine presence.

The expansion and elevation of professional elder care is one of the most morally urgent economic projects of the coming decades. It will require both the development of professional pathways that make elder care a genuinely attractive career — with compensation, status, and professional development appropriate to the importance of the work — and a cultural shift in how we value the care of the aged. A civilization's relationship to its elders is one of the most revealing indicators of its values. How we treat the most vulnerable among us, in the moment when they need us most, is who we are. The economy of the future should be organized, in significant part, around getting this right.

III. The Creative and Artisanal Renaissance

Alongside the care economy, the second major domain of expanding human economic activity in the age of AI is what might be called the Creative and Artisanal Renaissance: the explosion of demand for human-made objects, human-performed experiences, and human-generated creative work that carries the unmistakable signature of individual human intention and craft.

This renaissance is not a nostalgic retreat. It is an economic and cultural response to a genuine scarcity: in a world flooded with algorithmically generated content, machine-produced objects, and automated experiences, the things that bear the authentic marks of a specific human being's attention, decision-making, and care are becoming correspondingly rarer and more valuable. The creative practitioner of the post-AI era is not competing with machines on the grounds of technical perfection. They are offering something categorically different: the evidence of human presence.

The Economics of Authenticity

We are already seeing the initial stages of this renaissance, and its economic logic is becoming clearer. The market for handmade goods — furniture, ceramics, textiles, jewelry, food, beverages — has been growing consistently across the developed world, even as (or precisely because) the market for manufactured equivalents has been saturated. The premium for 'handmade' or 'artisanal' products reflects not merely a preference for quality — though quality is often higher — but a genuine hunger for the human connection that mass production, and now AI-generated content, systematically denies.

This hunger is not merely sentimental. It reflects a deep and accurate intuition about the nature of value that the Church of the Grind never adequately captured. When you buy a handmade object, you are not just buying an object. You are buying the hours of a specific human being's attention — the decisions they made in the making, the problems they encountered and solved, the intelligence of their hands. You are, in a meaningful sense, in a relationship with that person. And in a world increasingly mediated by algorithms, intermediated by platforms, and optimized for efficiency, this form of direct human-to-human value exchange is becoming one of the things people are most willing to pay for.

The economic implications are significant. A ceramicist whose work is distinctive, whose making process is visible, and whose relationship with their customers is genuine can command prices that would have seemed implausible in an era dominated by mass production. A small-batch food producer whose story is authentic and whose product reflects genuine craft can build a customer base that is loyal beyond what rational economic analysis would predict. A musician who performs live, who is present in their community, and who offers their audience the experience of genuine human presence and risk can sustain a career that the recorded music industry would classify as marginal but that provides a genuinely good and meaningful livelihood.

THE PERFORMING ARTS IN THE AGE OF PERFECT SIMULATION

The performing arts occupy a special place in the Creative and Artisanal Renaissance because they are the domain where the irreplaceability of genuine human presence is most immediately and viscerally apparent.

A live concert cannot be fully replicated by even the highest-quality recording. A live theatrical performance cannot be substituted by even the most technically accomplished film. These are not merely aesthetic preferences — they reflect something real about the phenomenology of live performance: the experience of being in the same space as another human being who is taking a genuine risk, exercising genuine skill under genuine pressure, and creating something that exists only in this moment, between this performer and this audience, and that will never exist again in exactly this form.

This is the irreducible gift of live performance: not perfection, but presence. Not the elimination of risk, but the shared experience of risk.

The performer who stumbles and recovers, who reaches for a note and barely catches it, who makes a choice in the moment that surprises even themselves — this performer offers the audience something that no recorded or simulated performance can provide: the authentic experience of human beings doing something difficult in the presence of other human beings.

The age of AI, paradoxically, may be the best thing that has happened to the performing arts in decades. As perfect recordings become free and ubiquitous, as AI can generate technically flawless musical performances on demand, the one thing that cannot be generated or automated is the live moment — the specific evening in the specific room with the specific performers and the specific audience. The economics of live performance, which have been under pressure from recorded media for a century, may be about to reverse. Scarcity creates value. And genuine human presence, in a world of automated abundance, is becoming genuinely scarce.

The Maker Movement as Civilization

Beyond the professional creative, the Creative and Artisanal Renaissance encompasses a broader cultural shift — what might be called the Maker Movement as Civilization. This is the growing recognition, across many different communities and contexts, that the act of making things with one's hands is not merely a hobby or a nostalgic affectation, but a fundamental human need whose systematic neglect in industrial and post-industrial societies has produced real psychological and social costs.

The evidence for this recognition is visible in the proliferation of maker spaces, craft studios, community workshops, and DIY communities across the developed world. It is visible in the renewed cultural interest in cooking, baking, fermentation, brewing, and other forms of domestic craft that were, a generation ago, systematically replaced by convenience food and professional services. It is visible in the explosion of online communities devoted to the sharing of making skills — from woodworking to fiber arts to metalworking to the countless other crafts that embody what Matthew Crawford beautifully calls 'the intelligence of the hands.'

What these communities understand, often without articulating it in these terms, is something that the analysis of this book has been building toward: that the act of making and engaging with physical materials, of solving the specific problems that a specific material poses, of developing skill through sustained practice with real-world consequences — provides something that screen-based activity, however stimulating, cannot. It provides direct, immediate, unmediated feedback about the quality of one's attention and skill. It provides the experience of genuine competence — of doing something difficult well. And it provides the satisfaction of producing something that exists independently of the process of its making — something that can be held, used, given away, that outlasts the moment of its creation.

In the age of AI, the Maker as a professional and cultural category will become increasingly important — not because manual craftsmanship will dominate the economy in the way that knowledge work did, but because the values it embodies and the human needs it serves will become correspondingly more central to the project of living a genuinely good life.

IV. Teaching, Mentorship, and the Transmission of Wisdom

A third domain of expanding human value is one that has always been among the most important human activities, even when it was not always among the most highly compensated: the teaching, mentorship, and intergenerational transmission of knowledge, skill, and wisdom.

AI systems can transmit information with extraordinary efficiency. They can explain concepts, provide examples, answer questions, and adapt their explanations to the apparent level of the learner with a consistency that no human teacher can match across thousands of simultaneous interactions. In this sense, AI is already transforming education, and the transformation will accelerate. For the delivery of structured information — facts, concepts, procedures, standard problem-solving techniques — AI tutors will, in many contexts, outperform human teachers.

But the transmission of wisdom — as opposed to information — is something that AI systems cannot yet do, and may never be able to do fully. Wisdom is not a database of correct answers. It is a disposition — a way of approaching problems, of balancing competing considerations, of knowing when the rules apply and when they do not, of remaining humble about what one doesn't know while being decisive about what one must do. Wisdom is acquired through experience, through failure, through the long, slow accumulation of perspective that only time and genuine engagement with life's complexity can provide.

WHAT WISDOM ACTUALLY IS

It is worth pausing on this question — what wisdom is — because it is one that our culture, with its emphasis on information and expertise, tends to under examine.

Wisdom is not merely accumulated knowledge. A person can know a great deal and be profoundly unwise. Wisdom is not merely intelligence. Some of the most intelligent people in any field make decisions of extraordinary stupidity in other domains of their lives. Wisdom is not even merely experienced. A person can accumulate decades of experience in a specific domain and remain stubbornly unable to generalize from that experience to related situations.

Wisdom is, rather, a quality of perspective — a way of holding one's knowledge and experience that is simultaneously confident and humble, decisive, and open. The wise person knows what they know and what they don't. They know the difference between the situations that their experience has prepared them for and the situations that require something new. They know when the standard approach is adequate and when it will fail. And they have developed, through sustained engagement with the full complexity of life — its successes and failures, its joys and griefs, its surprises, and disappointments — the capacity to hold that complexity without being paralyzed by it.

This quality of perspective is acquired through a specific kind of experience: experience that has been genuinely engaged with, genuinely reflected upon, and genuinely integrated into a developing understanding of what matters and why. It cannot be shortcut by processing more data. It cannot be replicated by training on the recorded outputs of wise people because the outputs of wisdom are not wisdom — they are the residue of a process that was always internal, always embodied, always irreducibly personal.

The Mentor as the Most Valuable Person in the Room

In the age of AI, the mentor — the person who has lived enough, failed enough, and reflected enough to have genuine wisdom to transmit, and who is willing to invest that wisdom in the development of someone younger or less experienced — is not a relic of a pre-technological past. They are one of the most valuable kinds of people in the world.

This is a claim that runs against the grain of how professional development has typically been understood in the knowledge economy. In the Church of the Grind, the most valuable professional was the one with the most current, most specialized, most technically sophisticated expertise. The mentor was often seen as someone past their professional peak — someone whose specific technical knowledge was no longer innovative, who was being kept on for their institutional memory and their ability to train the next generation while the younger, more technically capable practitioners were creating the real value.

This understanding is being inverted by the AI revolution. As the technical content of expertise is absorbed by AI systems, the residue — what remains when the technical scaffolding is removed — is precisely wisdom: the contextual judgment, the ethical discernment, the capacity for genuine relationship, the understanding of how things work in the full complexity of real human situations, that only years of genuine engagement can produce. And this is exactly what the mentor has to offer.

Consider what a genuinely wise mentor provides that an AI system cannot. They can tell you not just what the correct decision is in each situation, but why it is correct — what values it honors, what it trades off, what it says about the kind of professional and human being you want to be. They can see your specific blindspots — the patterns in your behavior that you cannot see from inside your own perspective — and name them with the combination of honesty and care that only genuine relationship makes possible. They can share, through the vulnerability of genuine disclosure, the specific failures, and confusions of their own development

— the moments when they got it wrong, what it cost them, and what they learned. And they can hold, with patience and without alarm, the confusion and incompetence of your development, because they have been there themselves.

These are not things that a language model can do, however sophisticated. They require a being who has lived through something — who has the specific scar tissue that comes from genuine failure in a domain where the stakes were real. And they require a being who has made a specific, costly commitment to the person they are mentoring: who is there not because their algorithm recommended it, but because they chose to be.

The Teacher as Cultural Steward

Beyond the individual mentorship relationship, the teaching profession itself — understood in its broadest sense — occupies a place of vital importance in the New Professions of Meaning. Not because AI will not transform teaching — it will, profoundly — but because the transformation will reveal, rather than eliminate, what teaching has always been most essentially about.

The most important things that teachers do cannot be automated: they model what it looks like to be genuinely curious, genuinely engaged, and genuinely committed to understanding. They create the conditions — the relationships of trust, the shared projects, the intellectual community — within which genuine learning becomes possible. They help students discover not just what to think but how to think: how to hold a question patiently, how to recognize the difference between genuine understanding and the performance of understanding, how to engage with ideas that challenge their existing beliefs without either dismissing those ideas or being destabilized by them.

These are cultural and relational practices. They are transmitted through modeling and relationship, not through instruction. The teacher who embodies genuine intellectual curiosity teaches students to be genuinely intellectually curious — not by explaining what intellectual curiosity is, but by demonstrating it in every class, in every conversation, in every moment when they encounter an idea that surprises or challenges them and respond with interest rather than defensiveness.

In the age of AI, the teacher's role as a cultural steward — as the living embodiment of the values and practices of genuine learning — becomes more important, not less. As AI systems take over the delivery of information and the testing of procedural knowledge, the teacher is freed to focus on exactly this kind of cultural transmission. The classroom of the future is less a place where information is delivered and more a place where human beings practice — together, in each other's presence — the specific skills and dispositions of genuine intellectual life.

V. Community Architecture and Social Infrastructure

The fourth domain of expanding human value in the age of AI is one that has received less attention in most discussions of the future of work, but whose importance is becoming increasingly clear: the building, maintenance, and stewardship of human community.

Community — genuine community, the kind of sustained, face-to-face, mutually committed social structure within which human beings have always done their most important living — does not maintain itself. It requires the deliberate, sustained labor of specific people who have committed themselves to its creation and preservation. It requires the organizing of gatherings, the navigation of conflicts, the cultivation of relationships between people who would not otherwise encounter each other, the telling of stories that give the community its sense of shared identity and purpose, and the holding of institutional memory that allows a community to learn from its past rather than repeating its mistakes.

This labor is, at present, entirely invisible economically. It is performed by volunteers, by people who choose to invest their time and energy in community not because they are paid to do so but because they understand, on some level, that the quality of their community is one of the most important determinants of the quality of their life. Community organizers, neighborhood association leaders, religious leaders, recreational sports league managers, local cultural event organizers —

these people perform labor of extraordinary social value that the market has entirely failed to compensate.

The Community Architect

As the dissolution of work-based identity accelerates, and as more people find themselves with the time, the need, and the motivation to invest in genuine community, the role of the Community Architect — the person who deliberately designs and tends the social structures within which human flourishing happens — will become more economically visible and more culturally valued.

The Community Architect works at the intersection of several domains: they need the relational intelligence to understand what various kinds of people need from a community, and how to bring those needs into productive relationship with each other. They need the organizational intelligence to create and maintain the structures — physical spaces, regular gatherings, shared projects, communication channels — that give community a skeleton it can inhabit. They need the narrative intelligence to tell the community's story in ways that deepen its members' sense of shared identity and purpose. And they need the conflict resolution skills to navigate the inevitable disagreements, power dynamics, and personality clashes that arise whenever human beings try to do something important together.

These are not skills that can be automated. They are not even primarily informational skills — they are relational and practical, developed through years of doing the actual work of community in specific places with specific people. And as the atomization produced by digital life, remote work, and the dissolution of traditional community structures intensifies, the person who knows how to build genuine community — who can take a group of isolated individuals and, through patient, sustained relational work, turn them into people who know each other, trust each other, and care about each other's wellbeing — is performing a service of incalculable value.

THE SPIRITUAL DIRECTOR AND THE EXISTENTIAL GUIDE

Closely related to the Community Architect is a role that is even less recognized in most secular discussions of work's future: the Spiritual Director, or what we might more broadly call the Existential Guide.

The Identity Crash is, at its depths, an existential crisis — a disruption not just of economic circumstance but of meaning, purpose, and identity. People navigating it need more than career counseling or financial planning. They need someone who can help them grapple with the fundamental questions that the crisis raises: Who am I if I'm not my job? What does my life mean if my work can be done by a machine? What do I owe myself, and what do I owe others, in a world that is changing faster than my capacity to adapt?

These are not questions that therapists are typically trained to address — though good therapists do address them. They are not questions that clergy are always equipped to address — though good clergy do. They are questions at the intersection of psychology, philosophy, and spirituality, and they require a guide who is comfortable in all three domains: who can accompany a person through the practical and emotional dimensions of the crisis while also holding open the larger questions about meaning, value, and purpose that the crisis raises.

The Existential Guide of the post-AI era might take many forms: the chaplain who accompanies people through major life transitions, the coach who works at the intersection of professional development and personal meaning, the spiritual director who helps people develop a contemplative relationship with their own inner life, the philosopher-practitioner who brings genuine philosophical rigor to the practical questions of how to live. What unites them is their commitment to accompanying people through the genuinely tough questions — the ones that have no algorithmic answers — and their willingness to be present to the full complexity and beauty of another person's struggle.

VI. THE ADVOCATE AND THE WITNESS

There is a fifth domain of human value in the post-AI economy that is the most politically and morally charged: the work of advocacy, justice, and bearing witness to what is happening to human beings in the age of intelligent machines.

The transition underway is producing, and will continue to produce, human casualties: people whose skills have been rendered economically obsolete faster than they can retrain, communities whose economic foundations have been dissolved by automation, individuals whose sense of identity and purpose has been so thoroughly disrupted that they are experiencing genuine psychological crisis. These people need advocates — people who can name what is happening to them, represent their interests in the systems that are making consequential decisions about their lives, and bear witness to the human cost of a transition that is driven primarily by economic and technological logic rather than by attention to human flourishing.

THE POLICY TRANSLATOR

One specific form of advocacy that will be increasingly important in the post-AI economy is what might be called the Policy Translator: the person who can move between the technical realities of AI development, the economic consequences of automation, and the lived experience of the people most affected by these developments — and who can translate fluently among these different registers.

The policy debates around AI and automation are currently impoverished in a specific way: they tend to be dominated either by technical experts who understand the systems but not the human consequences, or by advocates who understand the human consequences but not the systems. The Policy Translator occupies the space between these two positions — bringing enough technical understanding to engage credibly with the experts, and enough human understanding to represent the lived experience of those who are most affected.

This role requires, in its essence, the same capacity that this book has been arguing is the core of post-utility human value: the ability to hold technical and human knowledge together, to ask not just what the systems can do but what they should do, to resist the seduction of efficiency arguments when they come at the cost of human dignity, and to insist —

patiently, persistently, and with the specificity that comes from genuine knowledge of specific situations — that the people behind the data deserve to be taken seriously.

THE JOURNALIST AS WITNESS

The journalist — the person who goes to the places where important and difficult things are happening, talks to the people who are most affected, and brings back a truthful account of what they found — occupies a specific and irreplaceable position in the ecosystem of human value in the post-AI era.

AI systems can generate enormous quantities of content that resembles journalism. They can summarize reports, aggregate information, and produce readable accounts of events at a speed and scale that no human journalist can match. What they cannot do is go somewhere, be present, earn the trust of people whose trust is difficult to earn, witness something that has not been previously described, and bring back from that witnessing an account that is truthful in the specific, hard-won sense that genuine journalism aspires to — an account that honors the complexity of what was actually there, the humanity of the people involved, and the moral weight of what happened.

This is a form of knowledge that is acquired through the specific practice of showing up — of being physically present in the place where things are happening, being willing to be changed by what you encounter there, and having the craft and the courage to render what you found in a form that does justice to it. It is, in the deepest sense, an act of love: love for the truth, love for the people whose lives are being reported, and love for the readers who deserve to know what is happening in the world they share.

In an era of AI-generated content, this kind of witness journalism becomes more, not less, essential. As the volume of content increases exponentially, the ability to distinguish what is genuine from what is fabricated, what is true from what is merely plausible, what matters from what merely attracts attention — becomes one of the most important capacities a society can have. The journalist who has this capacity, and who exercises it with integrity, is performing a service to democracy and to truth that no algorithm can replicate.

VII. The Question of Compensation

Any honest discussion of the New Professions of Meaning must grapple with a tricky question: if these forms of human work are as valuable as this chapter argues, why are so many of them so poorly compensated?

The answer has several dimensions. Some of it is historical inertia: the compensation structures of the knowledge economy were built around the scarcity of specific cognitive skills, and those structures do not automatically adjust to reflect the new scarcity landscape that AI is creating. Some of it is political: the workers most concentrated in the care economy, the creative economy, and the community-building economy have historically had less political power than the workers in the industries whose compensation they are challenging. And some of it is ideological: the Church of the Grind has never been good at pricing things that resist quantification, and the most genuinely human forms of value are precisely the ones that resist it most stubbornly.

But the structural forces are moving in the direction of revaluation. As AI absorbs more of the cognitive labor that has commanded premium wages, the care, creative, and wisdom-transmission work that AI cannot absorb becomes correspondingly scarcer relative to demand. Scarcity drives compensation when the market for a service is functioning. And for many of the services in the New Professions of Meaning — from mental health care to skilled craftsmanship to genuine mentorship — demand is rising faster than supply.

The more important question may not be about compensation at all, but about sufficiency. The New Professions of Meaning may not generate the kind of wealth that the peak of the knowledge economy produced. They may require, in many cases, a genuine renegotiation of what constitutes enough — what material standard of living is required for a life of genuine flourishing, as opposed to the standard of life that the aspirational culture of the Grind has trained us to pursue.

This is not a counsel of resignation or acceptance of poverty. It is an invitation to a more honest examination of the relationship between income and wellbeing. The research is consistent: above a moderate threshold of material security, increases in income produce diminishing returns in subjective wellbeing. What predicts wellbeing above that threshold is not more money but more meaningful work, more genuine connection, more time for the activities that provide genuine engagement and satisfaction. The New Professions of Meaning may offer less of the former and more of the latter.

VIII. The Integrated Life: Beyond Work as Identity

There is a final dimension of the New Professions of Meaning that this chapter has been building toward but has not yet named directly. The transition from the Church of the Grind to a world where meaning is distributed across care, craft, community, and wisdom does not merely change what people do for a living. It changes the relationship between what one does for a living and who one is.

In the age of the knowledge economy, the most culturally aspirational identity was the one most thoroughly colonized by professional life. The person who worked hardest, who had the most impressive title, who had sacrificed the most of their personal life to their professional achievement — this person was, in the cultural imagination of the Grind, the most admirable. The rest of life — family, friendship, community, craft, contemplation — was what you did with the time that your professional life had not yet claimed.

The New Professions of Meaning invert this hierarchy. They point toward what might be called the Integrated Life: a life in which professional work is one important but not overwhelming dimension of a full human existence, and in which the other dimensions — the care one gives and receives, the craft one develops, the community one builds, the wisdom one accumulates and transmits — are valued not as supplements to professional achievement but as its moral and psychological foundation.

The person who brings genuine care to their professional work does so because they have genuine care in their life. The counselor who serves their clients well does so because they have genuine relationships from which they draw the empathy and wisdom their clients need. The craftsperson who makes something beautiful does so because they have developed, through sustained practice, the kind of attention to the world that beauty requires. The teacher who genuinely inspires their students does so because they are themselves genuinely alive to the subjects they teach — because their own life contains the curiosity, the wonder, and the engagement with difficulty that they are trying to cultivate in others.

The New Professions of Meaning are not, ultimately, about finding a new category of economically valuable activity to replace the cognitive labor that AI is absorbing. They are about recovering a richer, more integrated, more genuinely human conception of what work is for: not the production of outputs, not the demonstration of cognitive superiority, not the accumulation of credentials and compensation that prove one's right to exist — but the act of contributing, with the fullness of one's particular human being, to the lives of others and to the communities that make a genuinely human life possible.

This is the most radical claim this chapter has made, and the most important. The New Professions of Meaning are not a consolation prize for the cognitively displaced. They are the revelation, long deferred by the dominance of the productivity ideology, of what the best human work has always actually been. The AI revolution has not created a new category of human value. It has stripped away the categories that were obscuring it. What remains — what has always been there, waiting — is the extraordinary, irreplaceable, endlessly various reality of what human beings can offer each other when they are fully, generously, and courageously present.

A Note on the Transition

The New Professions of Meaning will not appear overnight. The economic and cultural structures that currently undervalue care, craft, community, and wisdom will not dissolve simply because the structural case for revaluing them has become clear. Transitions of this kind take decades, and they require not just economic adjustment but genuine cultural change — a shift in what we admire, what we aspire to, what we teach our children to value, and how we organize our collective life.

But the transition is underway. It is visible in the growing cultural interest in craft and making. It is visible in the renewed respect for care workers that the COVID-19 pandemic briefly produced — and in the frustration and grief of those workers when that respect did not translate into lasting change. It is visible in the explosion of interest in community, in mentorship, in the kinds of genuine human connection that the digital age has made simultaneously more necessary and more difficult to sustain.

The people navigating this transition — the ones reading this book, working out how to live and work with integrity in a world that is changing faster than our institutions can follow — are not simply adapting to economic disruption. They are, whether they know it or not, building the culture of what comes next. The choices they make about how to spend their time, what kinds of work to invest in, what they are willing to pay for and what they choose to offer — these choices, aggregated across millions of individual lives, will determine whether the post-AI economy becomes a world that genuinely values human beings or merely a more efficient version of the world that devalued them.

The New Professions of Meaning are a possibility, not a guarantee. They require the active, deliberate, sustained commitment of people who understand what is at stake and are willing to do the work — both the interior work of reimagining their own relationship to worth, and the exterior work of building the economic and cultural structures within which a more human-centered economy can function.

You are among those people. The work begins with you, and with the specific choices that are available to you in the specific life you are living. Begin there. Build from there. Trust that the small genuinely human things you contribute to the specific people and communities in your life are not peripheral to the larger project of human flourishing. They are, in fact, their substance.

CHAPTER TEN

CHILDREN, EDUCATION & THE NEXT GENERATION

✦ ✦ ✦

The most consequential question raised by the Identity Crash is not what it means for those of us who are already adults — already formed by the Church of the Grind, already navigating the difficult territory of reimagining our own worth. It is what it means for the children who are growing up in the middle of the transition, and for the educational systems that are supposed to be preparing them for their adult lives.

The children being born today will reach adulthood in a world whose economic and social structures we cannot fully predict. The jobs that will exist when they enter the workforce may bear little resemblance to the jobs that exist today. The skills that will be most economically valued may be entirely different from the skills that our current educational systems are most devoted to developing. And the psychological frameworks that will allow them to flourish — to find genuine meaning, sustain authentic relationships, and contribute genuinely to the world they inhabit — may be precisely the frameworks that our current educational systems are least equipped to cultivate.

WHAT SCHOOLS ARE CURRENTLY TEACHING

To understand the challenge, it is useful to begin with a clear-eyed assessment of what schools are currently teaching — not just in terms of explicit curriculum but in terms of the implicit curriculum that shapes what students learn about what matters, what constitutes success, and what kind of person is worth being.

Most school systems in the developed world are structured around the cultivation of exactly the cognitive skills that AI systems are most adept at replicating: the ability to absorb, retain, and reproduce information; the capacity to perform standardized cognitive operations with reliability and accuracy; the skill of working quickly and efficiently toward predetermined correct answers. These are the skills that standardized tests measure, that grades reward, and that the most prestigious universities select for. They are also, in the age of AI, among the least distinctive human capacities.

The skills that AI systems are worst at replicating — embodied intelligence, creative irrationality, genuine empathy, the capacity for sustained attention and deep engagement, the wisdom to navigate complex ethical situations, the ability to build and sustain genuine human relationships — are precisely the skills that most school systems treat as peripheral, unmeasurable, or simply not the school's job to develop. Physical education is a marginal subject. Art and music are routinely cut when budgets tighten. Social-emotional learning is often treated as an intervention for struggling students rather than as a core component of human development. Philosophy — the practice of thinking carefully about how to live — is entirely absent from most curricula.

What Education Needs to Become

The educational transformation required by the age of AI is not primarily a matter of updating curricula to include more coding, more data literacy, or more AI literacy — though these have their place. It is a much more fundamental reconception of what education is for.

Education, in the post-utility world, needs to be primarily oriented toward the development of the specifically human capacities that AI cannot replicate. This means, concretely, a much greater emphasis on several domains that are currently undervalued.

First, embodied intelligence and manual skill. Every child should have significant regular exposure to activities that develop the hand-mind relationship: drawing, woodworking, cooking, gardening, music, dance, athletics of various kinds. Not as extracurricular activities for those with aptitudes, but as core elements of human development that all children deserve access to.

Second, the cultivation of attention. The ability to sustain focused, undistracted attention on a single object or question for an extended period is one of the most important cognitive capacities a human being can possess — and one of the capacities most systematically eroded by the digital environment in which today's children are growing up. Schools should take the cultivation of attention seriously as an explicit educational goal: through sustained reading of long-form texts, through contemplative practices, through project-based learning that requires extended engagement with complex problems.

Third, genuine ethical reasoning. Not the rote learning of ethical rules or the application of predetermined frameworks to predetermined cases, but the actual practice of thinking carefully about tough questions that do not have easy answers. What do we owe each other? When is it right to break a rule? How do we make decisions under uncertainty? How do we weigh individual interests against collective ones? These are the questions that will define the most important decisions of the coming century — and the practice of thinking about them seriously is a skill that can and should be cultivated from an early age.

Fourth, the capacity for genuine relationship. This may sound like something that develops naturally, without formal cultivation. It does not — or not reliably, in a world where the default mode of social interaction for many children has shifted toward screen-mediated, algorithmically curated contact. The development of the skills of genuine relationship — attentive listening, honest self-expression, the tolerance of conflict and the capacity for repair, the willingness to be genuinely vulnerable with another person — requires practice, modeling, and a social environment that values these skills and creates space for their development.

THE ROLE OF PARENTS

For parents navigating the questions raised in this chapter, the most important thing to understand is that the changes required are not primarily about what you can add to your child's life — what additional activities, what additional screens, what additional structured learning you can provide. They are about what you can protect.

Protecting unstructured time — time in which children are not being managed, instructed, entertained, or optimized, but are simply free to play, to be bored, to discover what they are genuinely interested in when no one is telling them what to be interested in — is one of the most valuable things a parent can do in the age of AI. Unstructured time is the seedbed of genuine interest, genuine creativity, and genuine self-knowledge. It is also, in a world of relentlessly scheduled, screen-mediated childhood, one of the things that parents most need to actively preserve.

Protecting the experience of genuine difficulty — of allowing children to struggle, to fail, to experience frustration, and to discover their own capacity to overcome it — is equally important. The instinct to protect children from difficulty is natural and loving. But difficulty is also one of the primary sources of genuine competence, genuine resilience, and genuine self-knowledge. A child who has never been allowed to fail has never had the experience of discovering that failure is survivable — which is one of the most important things a human being can know.

And protecting genuine human connection — prioritizing shared meals, shared physical activity, face-to-face conversation, the kind of slow, present attention that makes a child feel genuinely seen — is the most foundational protection of all. In the age of AI, the most important thing a parent can give a child is not any skill or any knowledge. It is the experience of being genuinely known and genuinely loved by a specific human being who has chosen, again, to be present.

CONCLUSION

THE SECOND GENESIS

There is a particular kind of courage required to stand at the edge of what you have always known and to step forward into what you cannot yet fully see. It is not the courage of the battlefield, which is acute and adrenaline-fueled and has the clarity of emergency. It is the quieter, more demanding courage of the person who must rebuild their understanding of themselves and their place in the world — not in response to a single catastrophe, but in response to a slow, sustained, and comprehensive transformation that touches everything they have previously taken for granted.

This is the courage that the Identity Crash demands of us. And it is a demand that is also an invitation — the most important invitation that our species has received in several centuries.

The machine has taken the work. It has taken the reports and the analyses, the diagnoses and the briefs, the code, and the calculations. It has taken the ten-thousand-hour mastery that we built to make ourselves indispensable and rendered it, if not obsolete, then at least insufficient as the primary basis for a human identity. It has swept away the floor on which the Church of the Grind was built and left us standing in what feels, initially, very much like empty air.

But empty air, it turns out, is not where we are standing. We are standing, for the first time in the history of industrial civilization, on something far more solid: the actual ground of what it means to be human. The ground that was always there, beneath the cathedral of productivity we spent two hundred years constructing. The ground of embodiment and relationship, of irreducible subjectivity and creative irrationality, of genuine suffering and genuine care and genuine witness to the experience of other human beings in all their complexity and beauty and need.

The Identity Crash is not the end of human significance. It is the end of a particularly narrow and impoverished conception of human significance — one that reduced the astonishing, irreplaceable mystery of a human life to its measurable economic outputs. That conception served certain purposes, in certain historical conditions. It produced extraordinary material abundance, and that abundance is not anything. But it also produced, at enormous psychological and social cost, the chronic alienation, the epidemic loneliness, the quiet desperation, and the deep confusion about the purpose of existence that characterize so much of modern life even at its most materially comfortable.

We are being freed from that conception. Not by choice — the freedom is being imposed on us by a technological transition that we did not collectively decide and cannot collectively reverse. But freedom, however it arrives, remains freedom. And what we do with it is genuinely, consequentially, and thrillingly up to us.

The Second Genesis is not a guaranteed outcome of the Identity Crash. It is a possibility — one that must be actively chosen, deliberately constructed, and sustained against the very real alternatives of retreat into the Dopamine Trap, the bore-out of ghost employment, and the slow, quiet tragedy of the Uselessness Syndrome.

Who are you when you have nothing to do? You are someone who has always been there, waiting patiently behind the resume and the title and the performance review. Someone who has always had more to offer than any job description could contain. Someone who is capable of love, of craft, of genuine witness, of creative disruption, of embodied presence, of the specific, irreplaceable form of care that only a creature who has suffered can give to another creature who is suffering.

You are, in short, a human being. And in a world of intelligent machines, that is the most interesting and most valuable thing you can be. The crash is over. Now begins the life.

THE IDENTITY CRASH

How to Redefine Your Worth in the Age of AI

KEY TAKEAWAYS

✦ ✦ ✦

THE ARGUMENT IN FULL

Most books about artificial intelligence and the future of work are about the economy. They map which jobs will be automated, which skills will remain valuable, and which industries will be disrupted first. They are useful books, and they are not this book.

This book was about something the economic analysis cannot reach: the person inside the disruption. The human being who did everything right — who built the skills, earned the credentials, invested the decades of deliberate practice — and who is now discovering that the specific cognitive capacity they organized their identity around can be approximated by a machine. Not someday. Now. On a Tuesday morning, when the inbox is empty and the algorithm has handled the reports and the silence is louder than any alarm clock they have ever set.

The question that silence asks is the question this book has been trying to answer from its first page to its last: Who are you when you have nothing to do? What is a human life for, when the thing you have spent your life doing can be done without you?

These are not economic questions. They are existential ones. And they deserve an existential answer — one grounded not in productivity metrics or career strategy, but in the oldest and most consistently validated insights available to our species about what makes a human life genuinely worth living.

✦ ✦ ✦

THE FIRST MOVEMENT: THE DIAGNOSIS

The book opened with a diagnosis. It traced the history of how labor became identity — how the Industrial Revolution stripped work of its context, how the Protestant work ethic moralized what the factory had dehumanized, and how two centuries of compounding ideology produced the Church of the Grind: a cultural system in which a person's worth was synonymous with their productive output, and in which the absence of a task felt not like rest but like a moral failing.

This history matters because it reveals something that the disruption of AI is now forcing into visibility: the equation of worth with productivity was never a natural truth. It was a historical construction, built by specific people in specific circumstances for specific purposes. It served industrial capitalism extraordinarily well. It served human beings less well. And it is now being dissolved — not by a philosopher or a spiritual teacher, but by a language model that can write your reports, a vision system that can read your X-rays, and a generative algorithm that can produce code indistinguishable from your own.

The Efficiency Wall is the name this book gave to the threshold we have crossed: not the ceiling above which machines cannot rise, but the wall behind us, through which we cannot pass back. The Speed Gap is real. The death of the ten-thousand-hour rule as an economic guarantee is real. The Perfection Paradox — the strange phenomenon by which algorithmic perfection increases the market value of human imperfection — is real. The world has changed in ways that are permanent and not reversible by any amount of training, retraining, or professional development.

The Ghost in the Office is the human cost of this change rendered in its most poignant form: the person who is still employed, still receiving a salary, still attending the meetings — but whose core professional utility has already been absorbed by an automated system, leaving them to perform the elaborate ritual of work without its substance. Bore-out. Performative labor. The specific, socially invisible grief of a loss that has no funeral because it has no name.

THE SECOND MOVEMENT: THE ANALYSIS

The book's second movement examined the psychological mechanisms by which the Identity Crash unfolds in real human lives. The Worth Paradox: the more efficiently AI produces the outputs our economy values, the less necessary individual human beings feel — even as the world grows materially richer. Uselessness Syndrome. Contingent self-worth. The specific, devastating confusion of a person whose entire self-concept was built on professional cognitive performance, now facing a technology that performs those same cognitive operations faster, more consistently, and without existential need.

The Dopamine Trap was examined as the primary hazard of the transitional period: the algorithmically optimized digital attention economy, standing ready to fill every vacuum of purpose with a simulation of engagement that is real enough to provide temporary relief and sophisticated enough to make genuine recovery progressively harder. The slot machine mechanics of the infinite scroll. The neurobiological parallel between digital engagement and opiate tolerance. The feedback loop of sedation and shame that deepens the original wound with each cycle.

And the Human Renaissance was articulated as the possibility that the crisis makes available — not a return to the past and not a consolation prize, but a genuine reorientation of human value toward the domains where silicon hits a permanent biological wall. Embodiment: the irreducible knowledge that lives in a body engaging with physical materials and physical challenge. Irrationality: the creative wrong turn, the inspired intuition that contradicts the available data and arrives somewhere the data could never have predicted. Shared suffering: the ontological foundation of genuine empathy, available only to creatures who have themselves suffered, and therefore available only to us.

THE THIRD MOVEMENT: THE ARCHITECTURE

The book's third movement was constructive. It offered not a philosophy but a blueprint — the specific daily architecture of a life organized around human irreplaceability rather than market-valued cognitive performance.

The Deep Hour: one hour of purely analog engagement each morning, before the digital world is given access to your attention. Not because screens are evil but because the attentional system has been trained to orient toward stimulation, and training it back toward depth requires the same sustained, deliberate effort that any genuine skill development requires.

The Physical Anchor: a daily embodied practice demanding enough to require genuine presence. The body is the one substrate that is permanently, irreversibly, and proudly yours. No restructuring can automate it. No algorithm can replicate the specific knowledge that develops in a body that has met genuine physical challenge and discovered of what it is capable.

The Micro-Economy of Meaning: the deliberate construction of value through human-to-human exchange — the teaching, the care, the presence, the genuine community that creates a form of wealth no stock market can track and no machine can provide. The neighbor who shows up. The mentor who shares not just knowledge but the scar tissue of genuine failure. The friend who sits through the difficult night not because an algorithm recommended it but because they chose to be there, and the choosing cost them something.

Navigating the Transition explored the unglamorous middle ground between the old identity and the new one — the neutral zone where the grief is real, the disorientation is genuine, and the temptation to retreat into either denial or despair is constant. The Identity Inventory. The importance of witnesses. The specific psychological profiles of the Accelerator, the Avoider, the Nostalgist, and the Philosopher — and what each one needs to move through rather than around the transition.

The New Professions of Meaning mapped the external landscape: the counselor-professional whose value lies in human judgment rather than cognitive output, the care economy whose systematic undervaluation is being corrected by the same forces that are commoditizing cognitive labor, the teacher and mentor whose transmission of wisdom is irreplaceable precisely because wisdom is not information, the community architect whose work of building genuine human belonging is among the most important and least recognized activities available to a human being in the current moment.

And the chapter on children and education made the case that the most consequential question the Identity Crash raises is not what it means for those of us already formed — already navigating the difficult territory of reimagining our own worth — but what it means for the children growing up in the middle of the transition, and whether the educational systems that are supposed to be preparing them are preparing them for the world that actually exists.

What It Was Really About

All of this — the history, the diagnosis, the psychology, the architecture, the professions, the children — was in service of a single argument. An argument that is not new. That is, in fact, one of the oldest arguments in the history of human thought, advanced in various forms by Aristotle and Frankl and the Buddha and every wisdom tradition that has ever seriously grappled with the question of what makes a life genuinely worth living.

The argument is this:

Human worth is unconditional. It does not depend on productivity, on cognitive performance, on market value, or on any other form of external validation that the economy of any given era has chosen to reward.

This is not a reassurance or a platitude. It is a philosophical claim with a long and rigorous intellectual pedigree, and the current technological moment is forcing it back onto the agenda with an urgency that comfortable times have always allowed us to defer. The Identity Crash is not creating this truth. It is making it impossible to ignore.

The person who feels worthless because an AI can author their reports faster is not perceiving a truth about their worth. They are experiencing the collision between a technological reality and a historical ideology. Only one of those things is inevitable. The other was built — by specific people, in specific circumstances, for specific purposes — and it can be rebuilt differently.

The machine has taken the work. Not all of it, and not permanently from every domain — but enough that the old foundation is no longer adequate, and enough that the question of what else a human life can rest on has become genuinely urgent. This book has been an attempt to answer that question honestly, and with the full acknowledgment that the answer is demanding — that it requires genuine grief, genuine courage, and genuine sustained effort to inhabit.

But the answer exists. It has always existed. And the world we are entering — for all its disruptions, its losses, and its terrifying openness —

is, for the first time in the history of industrial civilization, actively creating the conditions under which that answer becomes not merely philosophically available but necessary.

The Five Ideas to Carry Forward

If you take nothing else from this book, take these five:

01 Your worth is not your output — The market's assessment of your cognitive productivity is information about the market. It is not a verdict about you. You were a person of full and unconditional worth before you had a job title, and you will be one long after that title has been transformed beyond recognition.

02 The most important things resist measurement — The quality of your attention to the people you love. The depth of your engagement with the work of your hands and your imagination. The wisdom earned through genuine failure and genuine growth. These are not peripheral to a worthwhile life. They are its substance.

03 The body is the ground — In a world where cognitive labor is being commoditized, the body — the breathing, moving, feeling, suffering, physically present organism that you irreducibly are — is the one substrate that no algorithm can replicate and no restructuring can devalue. Come home to it. Stay there.

04 Community is not optional — The research is unambiguous: the single most reliable predictor of sustained human wellbeing is the quality of genuine close relationships. Not wealth. Not professional achievement. Not cognitive performance. Relationships. Build them deliberately. Protect them fiercely. Invest in them as the primary economy of your life.

05 The crash is an invitation — The Identity Crash is not the end of human significance. It is the end of a particular and historically contingent form of human significance — one that was never adequate to the full dimensionality of what a human life can be. What it is dissolving is a cage, even if the cage felt like a home. What it is revealing is everything the cage was obscuring.

The machine has taken the work so that you can finally have the life. The crash is over. What remains is the question of what to do with the freedom — and this book's answer, from its first page to its last, is the same:

Everything.

AFTERWORD

✦ ✦ ✦

A LETTER TO THE FUTURE

By the time this book is read by most of the people who will read it, the landscape it describes will have evolved in ways that no one — including the writer of this book— can fully predict. The specific systems, the economic disruptions, the precise contours of the transition from the Church of the Grind to whatever comes next: all of this will be different, in ways large and small, from what these pages have described.

What will not be different — what is not, in fact, subject to revision by any technological development, however radical — is the fundamental situation of the human being who must navigate it. A conscious, embodied, relational creature, finite in time and breath, carrying within them the full archive of everything they have experienced, lost, and loved, seeking to understand what it means to be here and what it means to do that well.

To the reader who is in the middle of the crash: you are not broken. What you are feeling is appropriate. The disorientation, the grief, the sense of groundlessness — these are honest responses to a situation that genuinely deserves honest responses. Let yourself feel them. And then when you are ready — begin the work of building what comes next.

To the reader who is helping others through the crash — the therapist, the teacher, the manager, the parent, the friend: the most important thing you can offer is not answers. It is presence. The willingness to be genuinely in the room with someone who is genuinely lost, to not reach for the nearest reassurance, to trust that the human being across from you has the resources to find their way through this if they are accompanied rather than hurried.

To the reader who is building the systems that are driving the crash — the engineers, the entrepreneurs, the investors, the policymakers: the transition you are creating is real, consequential, and not going to be undone. But how it unfolds — how quickly, how inclusively, with how much attention to the human beings in its path — is not predetermined. It is a matter of choice. Make those choices with the full weight of that responsibility.

And to the reader who is simply trying to figure out what to do on a Tuesday morning when the inbox is empty and the algorithm has handled the reports and you are sitting before a screen wondering what, now, you are for: put down the screen. Go outside. Feel the air on your face. Notice something. Talk to someone. Make something with your hands. Read something that matters. Be there, completely, for someone who needs you.

You are not a productivity unit awaiting optimization. You are a human being in the middle of the most extraordinary transition your species has ever navigated. And you are more equipped for that navigation — by virtue of being exactly what you are — than any machine that has ever been built. Begin.

APPENDIX A

✦ ✦ ✦

THE IDENTITY INVENTORY: A GUIDED EXERCISE

The Identity Inventory is a structured reflective exercise designed to help you identify, articulate, and begin to inhabit sources of identity, meaning, and worth that are not dependent on your professional role or your economic utility. It is not a quick exercise. The full version, done thoroughly, takes several hours spread over multiple sittings. Most people who do it find it one of the most illuminating exercises they have ever undertaken.

The exercise is organized in five parts. Each part asks a distinct set of questions and invites a different kind of reflection. The instructions are to write your answers longhand, in a private notebook, without editing or judging what you write. The goal is not to produce polished prose but to discover what is there when you look honestly.

PART ONE: THE PROFESSIONAL SELF

Begin by writing, as completely and honestly as you can, a description of how your professional role has defined your identity. Include: what you do and how you have described it to others; what you are most proud of professionally; what professional accomplishments have felt most meaningful to you and why; what aspects of your professional identity you have most wanted others to see and appreciate; and what aspects of your professional self you have felt most anxious about losing.

Do not skip this part or rush through it. The point is not to critique the professional self — it is to see it clearly, in all its genuine value and its genuine limitations. You cannot release something you have not first fully acknowledged.

Part Two: The Pre-Professional Self

Now write about who you were before your professional identity became dominant. This may require going back to adolescence or even childhood. Who were you at ten years old? What were you most interested in, most passionate about, most naturally drawn toward? What activities could absorb your attention for hours without any thought of external reward? What did you want to be when you grew up before the Church of the Grind told you what was realistic?

Many people find this part of the exercise surprisingly emotional. The person you were before the professional self-took over is often someone you genuinely like — someone with enthusiasms, capacities, and interests that the years of professional formation have obscured but not entirely erased.

Part Three: The Relational Self

Write about your most important relationships — not your professional network, but the people you love and who love you, the friendships that have sustained you, the communities you belong to. For each relationship or community that feels genuinely important, describe: what you contribute to it and what it contributes to you; what you have learned from it; what it would mean to you if it were suddenly gone.

This part of the exercise often reveals that the Micro-Economy of Meaning is already more developed than you thought — that there are forms of value and connection in your life that you have been systematically undervaluing because they do not show up in the metrics that the Church of the Grind has taught you to track.

Part Four: The Values Self

Write about the values that have guided your most important choices — not the values you profess or aspire to, but the values that have genuinely determined your behavior when it mattered. You can identify these by examining the choices you have made that cost you something: the jobs you turned down, the opportunities you declined, the positions you took that made you professionally or socially uncomfortable. What were you protecting or honoring in those moments?

This part of the exercise often produces surprises. People discover that they have been guided by values they never articulated — a commitment to fairness that has shaped dozens of quiet decisions; a love of beauty that has influenced choices they described in purely practical terms; a deep investment in the wellbeing of specific communities that they have treated as peripheral to their 'real' life and work.

PART FIVE: THE IMAGINED SELF

Finally, write about who you would be if the economic and social constraints that have shaped your choices were suddenly removed. If you had sufficient financial security, and no concern for how others would judge your choices, and no lingering obligations to a professional identity you have already outgrown — what would you do? What would you make? What would you learn? Who would you spend time with? What problems would you try to solve?

This is not an invitation to fantasy. It is an exercise in discernment: a way of identifying what you genuinely care about, as distinct from what you have been trained to care about. The imagined self is not necessarily a self you should become entirely — real life always involves constraints and obligations that the imagination happily ignores. But the imagined self is a reliable guide to what you value most deeply. And what you value most deeply is where genuine meaning lives.

APPENDIX B

✦ ✦ ✦

Tools, Frameworks & Further Reading

The following resources have informed the thinking in this book and may be useful for readers who wish to explore specific themes more deeply. They are organized by the chapter themes they most directly address.

On the History of Work and Identity

Max Weber's The Protestant Ethic and the Spirit of Capitalism remains, more than a century after its initial publication, one of the most penetrating analyses of how the moral valuation of labor became embedded in Western consciousness. Alongside Weber, readers interested in the anthropology of work would benefit from Marshall Sahlins' Stone Age Economics, which contains the foundational analysis of hunter-gatherer societies as representing a condition of 'original affluence.'

For a more contemporary treatment of how work came to colonize identity in the twentieth century, Studs Terkel's Working — a collection of interviews with ordinary Americans about their relationship to their jobs — remains unsurpassed in its human specificity and emotional honesty. Richard Sennett's The Corrosion of Character examines how the shift toward flexible, project-based work in the late twentieth century began to undermine the stable narratives of identity that long-term employment had provided.

On the Psychology of Identity and Transition

William Bridges' Transitions: Making Sense of Life's Changes offers the classic framework for understanding major life transitions — distinguishing between endings, the 'neutral zone,' and new beginnings.

For readers interested in the neuroscience of identity and change, the research literature on 'contingent self-worth' — the attribution of one's value to performance in a specific domain — is usefully summarized in Jennifer Crocker and Lora Park's 2004 paper 'The Costly Pursuit of Self-Esteem,' published in Psychological Bulletin.

James Hollis's What Matters Most: Living a More Considered Life offers a depth-psychological perspective on the mid-life identity crisis that many people are now experiencing decades earlier than expected, thanks to the accelerated pace of economic change. His framework for understanding how the 'provisional life' — the life organized around external expectations rather than internal values — eventually collapses under its own weight is directly applicable to the Identity Crash.

On Artificial Intelligence and Its Human Implications

For readers who want to deepen their understanding of the technical and economic dimensions of AI's impact on work, Martin Ford's Rule of the Robots: How Artificial Intelligence Will Transform Everything provides a comprehensive and accessible overview. Kai-Fu Lee's AI Superpowers, while focused primarily on the US-China AI competition, contains some of the most thoughtful analysis available of which human capacities are most likely to remain economically valuable as AI systems become more capable.

On the philosophical dimensions of AI's challenge to human identity, Nick Bostrom's Superintelligence and Murray Shanahan's The Technological Singularity provide rigorous frameworks for thinking about the longer-term implications, while remaining, by design, agnostic on the psychological and humanistic questions that are central to this book.

On the Attention Economy and Digital Distraction

Cal Newport's Deep Work provides a rigorous case for the value of focused, undistracted cognitive engagement and practical strategies for cultivating it in an environment designed to prevent it. Johann Hari's Stolen Focus offers a broader investigation of the political, economic, and technological systems that are degrading human attention, with particular attention to the business models of the major technology platforms. Adam Alter's Irresistible: The Rise of Addictive Technology provides the most thorough account available of the specific design techniques by which digital products are engineered to capture and hold attention.

On Embodiment and Physical Practice

Matthew Crawford's Shop Class as Soulcraft: An Inquiry into the Value of Work is a philosopher's meditation on what it means to engage with physical materials and develop manual skill. John Ratey's Spark: The Revolutionary New Science of Exercise and the Brain provides a comprehensive review of the neuroscientific evidence for the cognitive and psychological benefits of vigorous physical exercise. Mihaly Csikszentmihalyi's Flow: The Psychology of Optimal Experience remains the most thorough and influential analysis of the psychological state that craftspeople, athletes, and skilled performers describe when they are most fully engaged — a state that is unavailable to AI systems and increasingly rare in the cognitively overloaded, digitally mediated lives of most contemporary humans.

On Community and Social Connection

Robert Putnam's Bowling Alone: The Collapse and Revival of American Community documents, with extraordinary empirical thoroughness, the decline of social capital in the United States. Sebastian Junger's Tribe: On Homecoming and Belonging is a shorter, more personal book about the human need for genuine community. For a broader perspective on the global crisis of social isolation and its health consequences, Vivek Murthy's Together: The Healing Power of Human Connection in a Sometimes-Lonely World — written by a former US Surgeon General — is both evidence-based and deeply human.

On Meaning and the Human Condition

Viktor Frankl's Man's Search for Meaning remains one of the most powerful arguments for the view that human beings can find meaning in any circumstances. Susan Wolf's Meaning in Life and Why It Matters offers a rigorous and accessible analysis of what makes a life genuinely meaningful. For readers interested in the spiritual dimensions of the questions raised in this book, Thomas Moore's Care of the Soul provides a depth-psychological framework for recovering the sacred in everyday life — one that is, despite being written before the AI revolution, remarkably prescient about the specific pathologies of meaning that the technological age produces.

ACKNOWLEDGMENTS

✦ ✦ ✦

Books, like human beings, are never made alone. This one is no exception, and the debts incurred in its making are as real and as meaningful as anything described in its pages.

To the researchers, philosophers, psychologists, and organizational theorists whose work forms the intellectual foundation of this book — to those who have spent their careers trying to understand what it means to be a human being in a world that is always, in one way or another, trying to convince you that your worth is equivalent to your productivity — thank you. Your work is not merely academic. It is genuinely life-saving.

To the many people who shared their experience of the Identity Crash in conversations, interviews, and correspondence — who were willing to speak honestly about the grief and the disorientation and the unexpected freedoms of this transition — this book is, in the deepest sense, yours. You made it real. I hope I have done justice to what you trusted me with.

To the communities of practice that are, quietly and persistently, building the Human Renaissance in real time — the craft guilds and maker spaces, the neighborhood associations and mutual aid networks, the reading groups and choral societies and community gardens — you are not peripheral to the story this book tells. You are its most important evidence.

To the educators who are already in classrooms and studios and playing fields and kitchens, teaching children what it means to be present in their own bodies, attentive to each other, and capable of making things with their hands — you are doing the most important work in the world. I hope something in these pages is useful to you.

To everyone who is genuinely trying to figure out what it means to be alive and human and valuable in a world that is changing faster than our hearts can follow: this book is for you. May it be, in some small way, useful. And not merely useful. May it be, in the way that the best things are, true.

www.ingramcontent.com/pod-product-compliance
Lightning Source LLC
LaVergne TN
LVHW050632100826
845148LV00011B/1844
* 9 7 9 8 9 8 6 8 9 7 6 3 9 *